SCOTTISH EDUCATION
SINCE THE REFORMATION

SCOTTISH EDUCATION
SINCE THE REFORMATION

R.D. ANDERSON

1997

© 1997 The Economic and Social History Society of Scotland

ISBN: 0 9516044 4 9

Cover illustration:
   The model school at Glasgow founded by David Stow in 1826. John
   Knox surveys the scene from his monument in the Necropolis.

Cover Design by Stevenson Graphics

Typeset & Printed by Stevenson (Printers) Ltd., Dundee ☎ (01382) 225768

CONTENTS

INTRODUCTION

This study, like others in its series, seeks to introduce the reader to recent research and interpretations, concentrating on academic studies since the 1960s. These are not as numerous as might be expected, given the distinctiveness of the Scottish educational experience. Two episodes have attracted special attention – the eighteenth-century universities, because of their significance for the Scottish Enlightenment, and the Education Act of 1872 – but there remain many large gaps, especially for the twentieth century. Education is often discussed in general works about Scottish history and politics, but research based on original sources has been patchy. Knox's brief survey of 1953 and Scotland's more ambitious work of 1969 were typical of an earlier tradition of institutional history: written by men working within the state system, at a time when educational history was widely taught in colleges of education, they tended to take a teleological view, seeing the landmarks of educational legislation as the logical culmination of a long development, and to neglect the social and political context.

This approach produced two special types of study. First, there were county histories, initially sponsored by the Scottish Council for Research in Education in the 1930s (Jessop, 1931; Simpson, 1947; Boyd, 1961; A. Bain, 1965), and followed by others on the same model (Russell, 1951, 1971; Beale, 1983). These effectively exploit the mass of local material such as kirk session and burgh records, though they seldom go beyond 1872; the best are those by Bain, Boyd, and Beale. Second, there are histories of individual institutions, especially the universities. All these have useful short accounts, mostly now rather aging (J.D. Mackie, 1954; Horn, 1967; Cant, 1970; Southgate, 1982; Carter and McLaren, 1994). No university has embarked on a large-scale modern history, but Aberdeen has published a series of studies to commemorate its quincentenary in 1995, which makes it currently the best-documented of the Scottish universities, especially for the modern period. There are also some

1

institutional histories of secondary schools, but few engage with wider educational developments, and they have been excluded from this survey.

Perhaps because the subject came to seem dry and old-fashioned, it was slow to benefit from the new approaches of social history, but it is these which now prevail. Results include a new emphasis on the experience of women, and the quantitative use of statistical evidence. In other countries, the history of education has begun to move beyond social to cultural interpretations, exploring its relation to the family and childhood, to literacy and popular culture, to religious practices and political consciousness, and to national and communal identity. The interest has shifted from supply to demand, from the systems shaped by elites in accordance with religious and political priorities to the meaning and uses of education for those at the receiving end. Such work remains limited in Scotland, and requires the exploitation of many new sources, but Houston's studies of literacy in the early modern period point the way.

Two particular problems face the historian of Scottish education. First, the British context. Although the union of 1707 did not immediately affect the autonomy of Scottish education, the developing role of the state in the nineteenth century and the response to industrialization brought the Scottish and English systems closer together. Many differences remained, and do so still despite assimilationist pressures, but to the outsider the common elements in British educational traditions are probably more striking. Explorations of the cultural differences within Britain have now begun (Robbins, 1988; Harvie, 1991), but historians of English education have seldom felt any need to look beyond the border, and Scottish education remains a blank in most general social histories which purport to be British. In some cases Scottish material has been usefully integrated into general syntheses (Stone, 1969; West, 1975; Paz, 1980; O'Day, 1982; Stephens, 1990; Sutherland, 1990; Smelser, 1991), but Sanderson's work on universities (1972, 1975) remains a rare example of the integration of Scottish and English research.

A second problem is that 'the superiority of the Scottish education system over that of England in the past as well as in recent times has been one of the pillars of Scottish self-esteem' (Whyte, 1995, 230). The historian has to deal not only with the realities of education, but with a meta-history of myth and idealization. Education has become a marker of Scottish identity, associated with various supposed

2

qualities of the Scottish character such as individualism, social ambition, respect for talent above birth, or 'metaphysical' rationalism. Older accounts of the educational system often saw it unfolding as the expression of a Scottish *Volksgeist*, from the days of John Knox onwards, and idealized the role of the 'lad of parts'. Historical analysis obviously has to test such myths against reality, but can also recognize that they are themselves a significant and sometimes creative historical force.

CHAPTER 1

Schooling in Pre-Industrial Scotland

Between the Reformation and the nineteenth century, education in European countries was a matter for church rather than state. Both Catholics and Protestants strove to evangelize the countryside and plant orthodox religion in the minds of its inhabitants, but stress on the Bible gave Protestants more concern for formal schooling and literacy. Scotland provides an early and sustained example of such an educational campaign. The state did not intervene directly, but gave statutory backing to the church's efforts, resulting in an unusually uniform and effective national system of parish schools. This was not affected by the union of 1707, which left education within the Scottish sphere, but the definitive establishment of presbyterianism in 1690, the end of the politico-religious disputes which had divided the elite in the seventeenth century, and the perceived need after 1715 to assimilate the highlands into the nation's political and religious culture, all strengthened and deepened the educational campaign. Only the advent of the factory and large-scale urban immigration at the very end of the eighteenth century cast doubt on its adequacy.

Traditional accounts of Scottish education lay much emphasis on the First Book of Discipline of 1560, in which the reformers proposed to establish a uniform system of schools at various levels, and on the legislation – in 1616, 1633, 1646, and above all 1696 – which sought to create the reality of a school in every parish. But achievement inevitably lagged behind laws and nationally-determined policies. Recent research has concentrated on patiently establishing the facts about schooling and literacy, social phenomena which have distinct histories. The two scholars who have contributed most to this work, Withrington and Houston, have not always agreed: Withrington takes an optimistic view of the extent of school provision in the early modern period, pushing back the date by which an effective school system was in place, while Houston challenges accepted views of

Scotland's superior literacy and stresses the lateness of universal literacy. But both switch attention to the grass roots, looking at what education meant to families, how they sought to satisfy their demands, and what the uses of literacy were.

There is no doubt that the reformers did have a vision of an educated people, though as with other aspects of their work there may be more continuity with late-medieval Catholicism than has been appreciated (Durkan, 1959, 1990). The new stress on religious life at parish level demanded both personal devotion based on reading the Bible and a learned clergy; local schools were linked to the universities through the teaching of Latin, and the recruitment of ministers was encouraged through bursaries, the seed from which the Scottish legend of the 'lad of parts' was to grow. To set up effective parish schools took many decades, but it is now generally accepted that in the lowlands nearly all parishes had a functioning school by the 1690s. The Act of 1696 consolidated this achievement rather than being a real turning point, but with amendment in 1803 it remained the legal basis of parochial education until 1872. The parish schools became deeply embedded in the rural community, and gave rural education a legal status and permanence lacking in most European countries, with teachers who were full-time professionals enjoying security of tenure. Local landowners (heritors) were required to build a schoolhouse and pay the schoolmaster's salary, and this obligation was regularly enforced. Although education was not compulsory, kirk sessions usually paid the fees of poorer children, and sending children to school became a part of community expectations. The superintendence of ministers and presbyteries, abundantly documented in the sources, meant that there was continual pressure to keep the system efficient, albeit pursued with more energy in some times and places than others (for examples, see A. Bain, 1965, 1989; Beale, 1983). By the end of the eighteenth century, the parish school was an ancient enough institution to attract idealization, and even nostalgia for a supposed golden age in the past.

In stressing the wide provision of schools, Withrington (1963, 1965, 1970, 1988b) was initially reacting against the gloomy picture in H.G. Graham's classic *Social Life of Scotland in the Eighteenth Century* (1899). Withrington's case is convincing, and stresses a number of points. First, the statutory schools were supplemented by private or unofficial ones about which the church-dominated records may be silent (for a Roxburghshire case-study, see Glaister, 1991). Private teachers opened 'adventure' schools for profit, or were paid salaries by parents who combined to set up a 'subscription' school; women ran 'dame schools' in their homes for girls and young boys; and in the most remote areas lads fresh from their own schooling boarded with families or circulated between them to give rudimentary instruction for a few months of the year. This ingenuity in using limited resources suggests that the desire for literacy already had strong popular roots.

Second, patterns of schooling were adapted to the rhythms of rural life and the seasonal demand for child labour. Full-time schooling was short – no more than four or five years, with attendance falling off sharply in the summer – but older children returned to study in the evenings and in the winter. The institutionalization of formal schooling, its substitution for the family as the main agency of socialization into community values, and the idea of a fixed 'leaving age' separating school and work were still in the future.

Thirdly, parish schools traditionally taught Latin, and the schoolmasters were expected to have some university experience. Even in 1690 Latin was widely available, and in subsequent years, as the economy expanded, both parish and private teachers branched out into subjects like book-keeping, navigation, surveying, and modern languages (Withrington, 1965, 1970). The wide availability of these useful and relatively advanced subjects, at moderate fees and in rural parishes as well as towns, was a distinctive feature of Scottish education, making its own contribution to economic improvement.

Finally, there were substantial regional and local variations within Scotland, still apparent when statistical information became available in the nineteenth century (Anderson, 1995). The most advanced areas were the borders and east-central Scotland; the north-east, later famed for its educational standards, lagged behind in earlier years. At the darker end of the spectrum were the highlands. But Withrington has challenged the view that highland education was uniformly backward, arguing that even in the seventeenth century the basic parochial structure was functioning (Withrington, 1986, 1988b). In the more prosperous districts this could work much as in the lowlands, though with scantier resources, and it was in the west highlands, both insular and mainland, that geography and poverty made education least effective; they were to be the last redoubt of illiteracy in the nineteenth century. The church saw the whole region as missionary territory, and the SSPCK (Society in Scotland for Propagating Christian Knowledge), founded in 1709, built up a network of subsidized schools; after 1745, highland education was promoted with new urgency as an instrument of political loyalty and economic development (e.g. the 'spinning schools' for girls). But churchmen saw literacy in English as the key to progress, and Gaelic was at first banned in schools, then allowed only grudgingly as an aid to learning English, creating a formidable cultural barrier between the family and the school (Withrington, 1962; Durkacz, 1983; Withers, 1984; Leneman, 1986).

The era of agricultural improvement released new resources for education in the lowlands: the ministers who reported on their parishes for the *Old Statistical Account* of the 1790s generally felt that popular education was in a healthy state, though they complained about the effects of inflation on teachers' salaries (Withrington, 1988b; Anderson, 1995). This broadly optimistic view of education and literacy on the eve of industrialization was endorsed by Smout in his general account of the period, whose chapter on education remains the best general synthesis available (Smout, 1972: but see also Whyte, 1995). However, just as the existence of laws does not guarantee the provision of schools, the existence of schools, even in some number, does not guarantee universal attendance or literacy, and Houston's work gives a more negative picture.

The spread of lay literacy in Scotland, starting at the top of society in the late middle ages, seems to have had nothing distinctive until the seventeenth century. Stone argues that it was then still below the English level, but after 1700 drew decisively ahead, a chronology which conforms with that of school organization. He estimates that male literacy around 1750 was 75% in Scotland, 53% in England (Stone, 1969, 120). It can only be an estimate, for the study of Scottish literacy suffers from the absence (until 1855) of the signatures in marriage registers which have formed the basis of most literacy studies elsewhere. It is impossible to establish chronological series of data even for specific towns or parishes. The value of Houston's work is that he finds signatures in other sources, though he provides more than one estimate of the overall literacy percentage: writing in 1982 he saw rapid progress in the late seventeenth century, with male literacy rising from 66% in the 1670s to 78% in the 1710s, then stabilizing around that figure until the 1750s (Houston, 1982, 90); in 1985, however, he cut the figure for the 1750s back to 65% (Houston, 1985, 56). Among weavers in Aberdeenshire around 1730, it was only 46% (Houston and Tyson, 1991). Houston also stresses the large gap between male and female literacy, no more than 25–30% of women in 1750 being able to sign their names.

Even 65% was a high figure for the eighteenth century, but it was certainly not 'universal' literacy, and Houston launched a stimulating attack on the 'literacy myth', stressing that in a comparative context Scotland was advanced, but not unique (Houston, 1982, 1983, 1985, 1988, 1989). Literacy rates in southern Scotland were similar to those in the adjoining counties of northern England. National boundaries and traditions may thus be less important than economic and social conditions, and even the traditional equation of literacy and Calvinism is called into question: Scotland fits into a pattern of high literacy characteristic of north-western Europe, but this zone includes Catholic areas like north-eastern France as well as Protestant ones like Prussia and Sweden, and Scotland seems less exceptional in this context than when compared directly (as is traditional) with England.

National literacy percentages are a crude measure, concealing wide occupational and regional variations, and the concept of literacy is itself far from straightforward. The transition from partial to complete literacy and from oral to written culture was prolonged, and eighteenth-century Scotland illustrates a situation where literacy and illiteracy could coexist within the family, and where reading was still an 'intensive' experience applied to familiar texts, especially religious ones, or a ritualized, semi-public activity, before becoming a private skill giving full mastery of the written word. By looking at evidence on such matters as book ownership and public libraries, Houston makes a start on the wider history of reading habits in Scotland (on which cf. Crawford, 1994).

Houston's work is most vulnerable to criticism in equating literacy with ability to write a signature. Most historians of literacy argue that the ability to read was the crucial achievement, and one which could be acquired outside formal schooling. Writing was a skill with much less social value, and 'reading-only' literacy was common in the transitional phase. In Scotland, there is much evidence that writing was taught separately: it was started later than reading, paid for at a higher rate, and often taught only to boys. Therefore it is likely that Houston's percentages underestimate the ability to read, particularly for women, and Smout has argued from his study of the Cambuslang religious revival of 1746 that reading literacy was almost universal in the lowlands (1982). One can perhaps conclude that lowland communities, if not all individuals in them, had passed the frontier

8

between oral and written cultures by the mid-eighteenth century. It was another matter in the highlands. At the Reformation literacy there hardly extended beyond the landowning class (Bannerman, 1983), and Houston's estimates for the mid-eighteenth century are very low; the highlands were one of the least literate regions of Europe – another reason for avoiding generalizations about Scotland.

Among the points investigated by Houston is the relationship between literacy and the socio-occupational hierarchy. Literacy penetrated downwards, and its progress can be measured by where the line was drawn. In the mid-seventeenth century, it had probably reached artisans, shopkeepers and small farmers; a century later, it embraced settled agricultural and urban workers, though the poor and rootless were still excluded. The migration and dislocation caused by industrialization, and the growth of a new working class, were to check this downward progress, and perhaps (though the data are too scattered to permit a definite conclusion) to reverse it: in the nineteenth century, heavily industrialized towns had lower literacy rates than the counties surrounding them, whereas previously (as normally in early modern Europe) the towns were more literate than the countryside. Houston shows that this was true even for a large and expanding city like Edinburgh (Houston, 1993). This superiority is all the more striking when, by comparative standards, Scottish rural education was so well developed.

Much more is known for this period about the parishes than the towns. The parish school legislation did not apply in royal burghs, but it was normal for town councils to maintain burgh schools. Unfortunately these have attracted very little research, not yet benefiting from the boom in urban history. There are useful conventional accounts in the county histories (Boyd, 1961; Bain, 1965; Beale, 1983), but there has been no real replacement for James Grant's *History of the Burgh and Parish Schools of Scotland*, published in 1876. Nevertheless, the outlines of the story are clear.

Burgh schools have a history reaching back to the middle ages, and few burghs were without them by 1600 (Durkan, 1959). Although their origins were sometimes in monastic or cathedral schools (including 'song schools'), they were essentially secular well before the Reformation. Town councils appointed the schoolmaster and paid his salary, which was supplemented (as in parish schools) by the fees paid by parents. The traditional burgh school was a grammar school, teaching Latin with an eye to the universities. Town councils had no legal obligation to provide education for all the inhabitants, though they often supported 'English' schools which taught reading and other basic skills, or gave small subsidies to private teachers. More significant were their attempts, as early as the seventeenth century, to meet the demand for modern and commercial subjects. This was done by appointing additional masters with their own schools, rather than by adding staff to the existing school. Most burghs thus acquired two or three schools, sometimes but not necessarily under the same roof, and parents could shop around between them. This system was distinctive to Scotland, contrasting both with the English grammar schools, which failed to adapt to new demands, and with the strongly organized elite colleges typical of continental countries. Also quite unusual was that girls were admitted to most burgh schools – though not in large numbers, and not in the university cities of Edinburgh, Glasgow and Aberdeen, where the demand for classical education was strong enough to allow the grammar schools to continue on traditional lines. For most parents, private schools with their domestic atmosphere remained the preferred option for girls.

There has been little study of the burgh school curriculum, though Camic (1983a, 1983b) argues that the 'universalism' of the Scottish Enlightenment's leading thinkers can be traced partly to their school experiences, when communal life and a rational curriculum laid the groundwork for emancipation from traditional Calvinism. The classical teaching in burgh schools changed in response to the progress of humanist scholarship, but its traditional prestige was challenged by initiatives like the Perth Academy of 1761, based on mathematics and science, which sought to provide local families with an alternative to the distant universities. Commercial expansion and a growing interest in science created an 'academy movement' which attracted the elites of many burghs (Withrington, 1970). By the end of the century, modernization of the curriculum usually went along with combining the various schools in a single building, often an impressive piece of civic architecture paid for by a public subscription; control remained, fully or partly, with the town councils, reflecting a sense that education was properly a public concern. Ayr and Inverness were early examples, and at Perth the Academy and Grammar School were merged in 1807; this movement continued through the first half of the nineteenth century. Even so, the different masters retained their autonomy, and it was not until after 1872 that the older burgh schools were turned into fully-integrated secondary schools (Anderson, 1985d).

10

Though the term 'secondary' was itself an innovation of the 1860s, the development of burgh schools tended to make them more socially and intellectually exclusive. As day schools they remained accessible to a wide social range, but once the provision of working-class education was accepted in the early nineteenth century as the sphere of churches and charities, town councils withdrew from this field. They had already abandoned their original power to license private teachers, and by the later eighteenth century parents in the larger towns had a wide choice. The profusion and variety of schools in Edinburgh, the only town to have been thoroughly studied (Law, 1965), was no doubt exceptional given its status as capital and university city. But private education, with social discrimination reflected in the level of fees, was very widespread in the nineteenth as well as the eighteenth century, and has been underestimated because it left few traces in the records. It lasted longer for the middle than the working classes, but most of the urban literacy discovered by Houston must have been acquired from private teachers, and arisen from spontaneous demand. It was in the towns, after all, that economic opportunities and social mobility made literacy seem most desirable.

Perhaps the opportunities opened to the middle classes by Scottish schools were more significant than those given to the poor, despite the myth (or 'fairy tale': Houston, 1985, 255) of the lad of parts. Social historians today are inclined to see early modern Scotland as an ordered and hierarchical society, firmly controlled by its landowners, clergy, and urban elite, who looked to education to serve the interests of loyalty, orthodoxy and social control (Whyte, 1995). Yet at least they put faith in education rather than ignorance as the means of preserving social stability, and within the framework of deference and patronage they were prepared to allow individual social mobility as a social safety-valve. Scotland possessed widespread literacy, cheaply available education above the elementary level, and (as we shall see) universities which were relatively accessible and linked to both parish and burgh schools. Traditional assertions about presbyterianism, democracy and the Scottish national character should be treated in a critical spirit, but there is a core of truth behind them. And not least of the church's legacies was the idea that education should form a single, national system under some form of public control.

CHAPTER 2

Universities and Enlightenment

By the end of the eighteenth century, universities and burgh schools shared a common context of urban expansion and prosperity, but there is a striking disparity in the historical attention given to them. University history has benefited from the burgeoning international interest in the Scottish Enlightenment, and no topic in this survey has attracted as much recent scholarship. The leading Scottish thinkers (with the notable exception of Hume) held university chairs, and the development of their thought can be studied from surviving lecture notes, whether their own or, more usually, those of students. The university curriculum can be seen as a direct expression of enlightened ideals of politeness, improvement and virtue. Many scholars, however, are primarily interested in the history of philosophy, political thought or science, and not in university history as such, or indeed in Scottish society.

Scotland had three universities founded in the fifteenth century, and the early years of Glasgow and Aberdeen have been the subject of distinguished recent scholarship (Durkan and Kirk, 1977; Macfarlane, 1985). The reformers wanted the universities to train learned, pious and orthodox ministers, but as with schools the impact of the Reformation was not immediate. It was the arrival of Andrew Melville from Geneva in 1574 to become principal of Glasgow University, then in a state of decay, which began the real changes (Durkan and Kirk, 1977; Kirk, 1994). The 'nova erectio' at Glasgow in 1577 was a model for reforms at King's College, Aberdeen, while Melville himself moved to St Andrews in 1580 to reorganize the teaching of divinity. The new spirit also inspired two new colleges: Edinburgh in 1583, under the control of the town council (Lynch, 1982), and Marischal at Aberdeen in 1593 – not combined with King's into a single university until 1860. These foundations reflected a continental protestant preference for urban universities, and Melville's policies have been seen as a weapon of the urban elite against the aristocracy (Kearney, 1970). His wider aim was to promote presbyterianism within the church; as a university reformer he encouraged the change from regenting (one teacher taking a group through the whole arts curriculum) to specialist chairs, and the replacement of traditional scholasticism by the modified form of Aristotelian teaching invented by the French Protestant Pierre Ramus. Other humanist influences included the strengthening of Greek studies. But 'Ramism' and the abolition of regenting were short-lived. At King's College, for example, where episcopalian forces remained strong, there was first a backlash against the Melvillean 'new foundation', then a further revolution imposed by the Covenanting regime in the 1640s (Stevenson, 1990).

A notable development in European universities in the Renaissance era was the influx of nobles and gentry, in search of legal training and a more polished general education. In England, for example, university numbers reached a peak in the mid-seventeenth century not regained until the end of the nineteenth. How far was this true of Scotland? From their origins, the universities had been intended to train servants for the state as well as the church. They had not been purely ecclesiastical institutions, and their affairs had attracted the intervention of crown and parliament, but their secular role remained limited. Although there were chairs in law and medicine, professional training failed to establish itself firmly (French, 1983; Cairns, 1994), and its potential was limited by the penchant of Scots for studying and teaching on the continent, not compensated by any large reciprocal movement. The Reformation disrupted these patterns, and Catholic universities like Paris and Louvain were now out of bounds, but their place was taken first by the Protestant academies in France, and then by Holland. It became common for the landed class to send their sons to study law at Leyden or Utrecht, and the popularity of the Dutch universities was at its peak between 1675 and 1750 (Feenstra, 1986). Numbers fell off sharply thereafter, reflecting the new vitality of the Scottish universities, whose own development of legal and medical education was strongly influenced by the Dutch model.

The loss of the court in 1603 and the absence of a continental-style bureaucracy meant that the link between university education and state office in Scotland was weak. There were signs of affluence in the 1620s–1630s, including the complete rebuilding which Glasgow embarked on in 1630, probably reflecting growing lay patronage as well as the new prestige of the clerical profession. Expansion was checked by the civil war and interregnum, but seems to have resumed after 1660, though this remains an ill-documented period. For nearly a century, the role of the universities in teaching correct religious doctrine put them at the storm centre of ecclesiastical and political disputes, and both the General Assembly and the state intervened periodically to impose reform of the curriculum and to purge the professoriate (C. Shepherd in Carter and Withrington, 1992: the best brief account of the seventeenth century). The universities suffered from such intervention in the 1690s, and again after the 1715 rising. But the post-1715 purge was the last of its kind, and by 1745 the universities had settled into Hanoverian loyalty.

They now became deeply embedded in the patronage system which regulated Scottish public life, and this has been studied in some detail (Emerson, 1977, 1992; Emerson in Hook and Sher, 1995). Directly or indirectly, the political elite was able to influence most appointments to chairs, and professors had close links with both national factions and local kinship networks. The other side of this was nepotism, chairs being seen as a form of property with rights of reversion, a system which at least preserved some academic autonomy. Often these factions had no ideological significance, but after 1750 division within the Church between moderate and evangelical parties made control of university chairs a vital issue; the moderate phalanx led by William Robertson (principal of Edinburgh University 1762–93) usually prevailed (Sher, 1985), and these struggles continued under different labels into the early nineteenth century. New ideas about merit and political impartiality then brought the reform of appointments, and the elimination of sinecures and nepotism (Anderson, 1987a). Yet the *ancien régime* arrangements had not failed to produce men of intellectual distinction.

There is no single definitive work on universities during the Enlightenment. What is available is of three kinds (there is a good bibliography in Sher, 1985). First, useful but mostly brief syntheses of current knowledge, none of them very recent (Cant, 1967; Chitnis, 1976; Emerson, 1977). Second, essays which integrate the universities into an interpretation of the Enlightenment as an elite response to the problems of Scottish society, notably those by Phillipson (1974, 1981, 1988). And third, specialized articles on particular universities, subjects, or professors: these are too numerous to be cited individually, though there are some collections which emphasize the universities (Campbell and Skinner, 1982; Carter and Pittock, 1987; Hook and Sher, 1995). For some reason, scholars in this field are more addicted to articles and essays than full-length books.

The curriculum is at the centre of interest. The final abolition of regenting during the eighteenth century, and its replacement by discursive lectures given in English, opened the way for the professors to discuss contemporary problems, and to imbue their charges with politeness and civic virtue, in a way which appealed to the professional and landed elite. New chairs were founded in subjects such as 'civil history' and rhetoric. The urban setting of the universities (apart from St Andrews, which remained very small while the others expanded) made them part of a thriving public culture; it was symptomatic that the more urban of the Aberdeen colleges, Marischal, was also the more lively. The towns gave many opportunities for sociability, including discussion clubs and societies at both elite and student level, while the professors themselves gave private classes outside their formal courses, and sometimes opened their lectures to the general public.

In Sher's words, 'the core of the eighteenth-century arts curriculum ... was the philosophy sequence of logic, natural philosophy, and moral philosophy. Mathematics and the ancient languages were regarded less as ends in themselves than as the necessary foundation for philosophical attainments. The chief objective was the production of well-rounded gentlemen, imbued with Christian humanist values and familiar with all branches of polite learning' (Sher, 1985, 29–30). The moral philosophy chairs lent themselves especially to this approach, and the Glasgow professor Francis Hutcheson (1730–46) is recognized as the pioneer (Stewart, 1990). One trend of recent scholarship, however, has been to switch attention from the golden age of enlightened thought after 1740, and to stress the continuity of the Enlightenment with earlier Scottish intellectual developments. There has been a reaction against Trevor-Roper's strictures on the backwardness of seventeenth-century Scotland and its universities' reputation as 'the unreformed seminaries of a fanatical clergy' (1967, 1636). Fanaticism was still alive in 1696, when the Edinburgh student Thomas Aikenhead was executed for blasphemy, but in the later seventeenth century, it is argued, Calvinism had generally proved compatible with intellectual progress, and the universities did not lag behind those of other countries in moving away from Aristotle and grappling with the ideas of Descartes, and then of Newton and Locke (see the essays by R. Cant and C. Shepherd in Campbell and Skinner, 1982). The reorganization of the universities owed much to the principalship of William Carstares at Edinburgh (1703–15), and by the 1720s was well under way; Hutcheson was not the only professor of his generation to adopt ideals of politeness (Phillipson, 1974; Jones, n.d., 1983; Duncan, 1987).

The perspective has also broadened from seeing Enlightenment philosophy as the 'science of man', making pioneering contributions to political thought, history, sociology and anthropology, towards stressing the breadth of Scottish enlightened thought. The teaching of classics is an aspect of the curriculum, and a central one, which is still neglected. But historians of science have long recognized the centrality of the universities for the development and diffusion of science (Morrell, 1971; Christie, 1974; Shapin, 1974), and have recently emphasized the links with the 'virtuosi' of the late seventeenth century, and the importance of mathematics and experimental sciences in the student curriculum (Emerson, 1988; Wood, 1988, 1992, 1993, 1994; Wood in Stewart, 1990, and in Hook and Sher, 1995).

By contrast with Oxford and Cambridge, the Scottish universities established themselves in the eighteenth century as schools of professional training. Cairns has illuminated the development of law teaching, at Glasgow as well as Edinburgh (1993a, 1993b, 1995; and in Hook and Sher, 1995), while medicine became a university affair in Scotland long before effective medical degrees were available in England. The medical schools which developed from the 1720s in Edinburgh, and to a lesser extent in Glasgow, were linked with hospitals for clinical teaching, and stimulated new chairs in subjects like botany and chemistry (Lawrence, 1985; Doig, 1993). Medical studies drove the expansion of student numbers in the late eighteenth and early nineteenth centuries (Rosner, 1991; Lawrence, 1988; Dow and Moss, 1988), and the professors of chemistry soon branched out into industrial and agricultural applications of their science, putting the universities at the centre of the practical, improving side of the Enlightenment which was part of its appeal to the elite.

Finally, recent work has criticized the Edinocentricity of earlier scholarship, and emphasized the independence and originality of intellectual life at Aberdeen (Carter and Pittock, 1987) and Glasgow (Hook and Sher, 1995; Sher, 1995; Butt, 1996). The Glasgow Enlightenment, it is claimed, has a practical character which laid foundations for the city's later industrial development. Glasgow intellectuals attacked older humanist traditions in the name of utility, and 'a commitment to the mechanical and fine arts as a legitimate component of a modern university may have been a unique feature of the Glaswegian Enlightenment during the eighteenth century' (Sher, 1995, 337).

Thus the Scottish universities, expanding from their core function of training ministers, developed a very modern combination of professional and general education. They had much in common with universities in other Protestant countries like Holland and northern Germany, and unlike those in France were the main channel for enlightened ideas to reach the educated classes. 'Nowhere in Europe had the universities been so responsive to social needs; nowhere had they provided so high a proportion of enlightened intellectuals or ones who so profoundly shaped the economic, social, religious and political life of their country' (Emerson, 1977, 474).

Whether it is also true that 'the low cost of university education ensured that any pupil of reasonable ability – the "lad o' pairts" of Scottish tradition – could proceed to a university without undue difficulty', or that Scottish society was 'permeated by libertarian ideas and democratic attitudes that blunted the inequalities of rank and influence' (Cant, 1967, pp. 1955, 1962) is more questionable. Recent historians (e.g. Sher, 1985) have preferred to stress the social conservatism of the Enlightenment thinkers, the concern of the curriculum with 'polite' ways of thinking and behaving, and the targeting of the enlightened reform programme at the decision-making elite. So is the 'democratic intellect' a myth? This phrase has been popularized by Davie, whose interpretation of the Enlightenment stands rather apart from the mainstream of scholarship. Davie argues that the generalism of the Scottish philosophical tradition was both a barrier to the atomistic individualism threated by industrialization, and a means of 'bridging the gap between the expert few and the lay majority', so 'building a sort of intellectual bridge between all classes': the Scottish intelligentsia remained in touch with its popular roots, and retained a strong sense of social responsibility (Davie, 1991, 59, 61: originally published 1973). Davie's case for the democratic intellect has always focused on analysis of the university curriculum, stressing the nature of elite education and the centrality of philosophy, not on the structure of educational institutions or on data about the social origins and mobility of students.

The latter are in any case sparse before the nineteenth century, and Mathew's work on Glasgow matriculation records (1966) remains the only detailed earlier study. Each university drew mainly on its own region (Smart, 1974), and at Glasgow the figures reflected the nature of the city: students from the landed class fell from 32% of the total in the 1740s to 7% in the 1830s, while those from 'industry and commerce' rose from 26% to 50%. Mathew claims that about a third of the latter group were 'working class' (mainly artisans), though the ambiguity of the original Latin descriptions makes this conclusion a tentative one, and few of the rural poor found their way to Glasgow. Among the occupations adopted by ex-students, the church headed the list – 45% over the whole period 1740–1839, with medicine at 13%, law at 8%, and industry and commerce at 12%. Teaching took only 6%, which suggests that the social role of the university was still restricted. Whatever the actual proportion of working-class students, the university was certainly being used by the expanding bourgeoisie, particularly those who wished their sons to move into the professions. The patronage of the mercantile elite differentiated Glasgow from the landed and professional tone of Edinburgh, but perhaps their gentrified sons did not return to the counting-house (Sher, 1995).

Our knowledge of student numbers is inevitably imprecise for this period. Cant has an estimate of 1,450 for c.1720 (Edinburgh 600, Glasgow 400, Aberdeen 300, St Andrews 150), and Emerson suggests that by 1800 they had risen to nearly 3,000. By the 1820s there were about 4,250 (Cant in Campbell and Skinner, 1982, 57; Emerson, 1977, 473; Anderson, 1983a, 347). There was thus very considerable expansion, and in a European context these figures represent a high ratio of places to population. This was possible because both parish and burgh schools could act as feeders. The age of university entry – usually 15 or 16, though it could be younger – seems to have remained stable from the seventeenth century until the nineteenth. Since this was also the usual age for entering a commercial or professional office, the burgh schools had virtually no older pupils; the universities were covering ground left elsewhere to secondary schools, and the modernization of their curriculum allowed them to beat off the challenge of the academy movement. Only basic Latin was demanded as an entrance qualification, and this in turn meant that entry was easy for boys from parish schools. The direct link between parish schools and universities was fostered, from the Reformation onwards, by bursaries designed to encourage entry to the ministry (Durkan and

Kirk, 1977). But one cannot assume that lads of parts came from really poor families; the Scottish professions drew on a popular base, but one which seldom fell below the level of tenant farmers, merchants and shopkeepers, or skilled artisans. This was certainly true of the university professors themselves, whose origins have been investigated in detail by Emerson (1992 – data covering all the universities; and in Hook and Sher, 1995). They came chiefly from the urban middle classes, though not from the wealthiest groups, about a third being sons of ministers. Their social profile was probably higher than that of the typical student because career advancement needed patronage and family influence, but it was to change very little in the nineteenth century despite the advent of meritocracy (Anderson, 1987a).

It should also be noted that certain 'open' features later thought characteristic of Scotland developed only in the eighteenth century. The new professorial system allowed a flexible curriculum with freedom of choice, formal graduation fell out of use, and students lived at home or in lodgings; the authorities took no interest in their private lives, and Scottish university education was an intellectual process rather than an Oxbridge-style community experience. But all this was new. Until after 1700 the colleges remained residential communities, with common tables and strict discipline, and students were expected to follow a fixed curriculum, involving elaborate oral exercises as well as the study of texts (for the example of Aberdeen, see Stevenson, 1990; McLaren, 1990, 1991, and in Carter and Withrington, 1992). One can perhaps conclude (as suggested by Withrington in Carter and Pittock, 1987) that the eighteenth century was an age when the social as well as the intellectual character of the universities underwent a formative revolution; and that if their social and institutional history were to be studied as intensively as their curricula, the popular as well as the elite side of enlightened Scotland, and its roots in widely diffused literacy, might come into sharper focus.

CHAPTER 3

Popular Education in the Nineteenth Century

The story of Scottish education in the nineteenth century is tradition-ally structured around the 1872 Education Act. Many older works end there, and give the impression of a direct transition from the parish schools to modern state education. The act made schooling compulsory, and put most schools under public control, administered locally by elected school boards and centrally by the Scotch Education Department (not renamed 'Scottish' until 1918). But this was only the culmination of an extended process of state intervention. Parish schools were strengthened by legislation in 1803, and survived with little further change until 1872, but the statutory system was not extended to the towns. There popular education became a field of action for voluntary bodies and churches, starting around 1810, and with the help of state subsidies from the 1830s. At first there were only modest building grants, but from 1846 schools received annual grants if they had state-certificated teachers and followed an approved curriculum. This 'privy council' system was supervised by the Edu-cation Department in London, founded in 1839, and by the Scottish-based inspectorate (Bone, 1968). By the 1860s most working-class children were being educated in these voluntary schools, which formed a semi-public system, and the task of the 1872 Act was to bring the voluntary and statutory sectors together, rationalize provision under a single local authority, and plug the gaps in universal provision.

This history was greatly complicated by Scotland's religious div-isions. In the 1820s and 1830s, church leaders like Thomas Chalmers hoped that state and church could work together, expanding the parochial tradition into the cities, and recreating there the paternal-istic relationships of the rural parish. Chalmers's own educational experiments in Glasgow and Edinburgh provided models, and he worked out a theoretical justification for state support which rejected laissez-faire ideology (Anderson, 1983b; S.J. Brown, 1978–80, 1982).

But the existence of strong religious minorities prevented outright state support to the established church even before it was split by the Disruption in 1843. The new Free Church ran its own schools, and the state had to divide grants impartially between all denominations, including Roman Catholics and Episcopalians. This denominational-ism, at its height in the 1850s and 1860s, was deplored by many Scots who sought the reestablishment of a unified national system. But the rivalry of the churches made this no easy achievement.

One product of the ensuing political manoeuvres was the commission of inquiry under the duke of Argyll, whose reports of 1867–8 provide the historian with a mass of information and statistics. Regular statistical inquiry was an innovation of the nineteenth century, and both the state bureaucracy and the churches collected and published such data. Annual reports, parliamentary debates, controversial books and pamphlets all make this period in some ways better documented than the years after 1872. Though an indispensable resource, the political context in which such sources were produced means that their accuracy and objectivity should never be taken for granted. Nevertheless, they underlie the general accounts of the period which historians have constructed (Withrington in Humes and Paterson, 1983; Withrington, 1988a, 1988b; Corr in Fraser and Morris, 1990; Anderson, 1995).

Such accounts, and corresponding local studies (Boyd, 1961; A. Bain, 1965; H. Hutchison, 1971), inevitably stress the complexity of the pattern, and it is difficult to disentangle the history of school provision from that of parties and ideologies. The earliest voluntary efforts were linked with propaganda for new teaching methods, and often provided model schools where teachers could receive rudimentary training. The infant school movement was one example (Roberts, 1972), but the great panacea of this early period was the monitorial method, which allowed one teacher, assisted by child monitors, to handle large numbers. The Lancasterian version was introduced into Scottish towns, and has attracted attention because of its special architectural demands, and because it seemed to express a new, Benthamite pedagogy based on the schematic classification of children, akin to the prison or the workhouse in its desire to control working-class lives (Markus, 1982). This foreshadowed modern state education more accurately than Robert Owen's celebrated but short-lived libertarian experiments at New Lanark (Donnachie and Hewitt, 1993).

Owen and the Lancasterian schools represented a phase of radical, secular thinking which faded as the churches became the main agencies of urban education. 'Sessional' schools associated with individual congregations on the model recommended by Chalmers were supplemented by district or mission schools which gave a more basic education to the poor (Hillis, 1987). The established church also took on the training of teachers, in 'normal colleges' in Glasgow (founded by the educational pioneer David Stow) and Edinburgh; the Free Church founded a duplicate set after 1843, and the state subsidized both. Creating a body of professionally trained teachers was seen as the key to improvement, and the post-1846 grants were linked to the pupil-teacher system: pupil-teachers were adolescents who served an apprenticeship as teachers while completing their own education, then competed for scholarships to continue their training at the colleges (Cruickshank, 1970). Since the supply of adult teachers lagged behind the expansion of schooling, pupil-teachers survived into the twentieth century.

Various types of urban school differed from the norm. There were Roman Catholic schools, whose history has been well covered (McGloin, 1962; M. Skinnider on Glasgow in Bone, 1967; Treble, 1978; Fitzpatrick, 1985). They did not make much progress until they started benefiting from denominational grants in 1848, and were always constrained by the poverty of the Irish working-class communities who were their chief clientele. There were charitable schools founded by endowment, usually offering free education (as state-aided schools were forbidden to do). There were the ragged schools, originally founded for street children, but evolving later into 'reformatory' and 'industrial' schools for truants and delinquents (Clark, 1977; Ralston, 1988; P. Mackie, 1988, 1992). There were also many purely private or adventure schools. Some of these flourished by charging higher fees and satisfying middle-class or white-collar needs, but private schools for the working class, once the main providers of basic literacy in the towns, declined before competition from the subsidized church schools. All these types of school, mostly small, charging different levels of fees, and attracting pupils on denominational and social criteria rather than serving a defined district, meant that the educational ecology of the cities was very complex.

It was in the large cities that the sense of social crisis was greatest, especially in the 1830s and 1840s. Fears that the working class was becoming impervious to religious influence led both clergy and laymen to see church-directed education as an instrument of moralization and social control, though it is impossible to disentangle these motives from humanitarian and evangelical ones. The slums were not the only missionary field, however, and there was a new wave of interest in highland education. From 1811 'Gaelic school societies' were founded in the lowland cities to support teachers in the poorer highland areas (Durkacz, 1983; Harding, 1980–2); in 1824 the Church of Scotland set up a scheme of General Assembly schools, initially directed at the highlands though later extended elsewhere (Chambers, 1975); legislation of 1838 paid for 'parliamentary' schools in some highland parishes; and the Free Church became very active in its highland strongholds (Withrington, 1963–5). Together these efforts brought substantial progress, and by the 1860s, as the Argyll report showed, high illiteracy was confined to the Hebrides. The 1872 Act, and the government policies which followed it, have commonly been contrasted with the earlier initiatives, and blamed for the decline of the Gaelic language (Macleod, 1960–3; MacKinnon, 1972; Smith, 1978–80). But this seems doubtful: before as after 1872, Gaelic was used only to accelerate the learning of English, and few dissented from the view that literacy in English was the key to ending poverty and bringing the highlands into the mainstream of economic development (Durkacz, 1977).

In the lowlands, only the smallest parishes relied on a single school, and the gaps were filled by 'side schools' (paid for by the heritors under the 1803 Act), church schools, subscription schools organized by parents, and schools subsidized by landowners. There was a special problem with factories and mines, which took children away from school at an early age. With the advent of steam, factories expanded in cities like Dundee and Glasgow as well as in many medium-sized towns, but the early water-powered cotton mills were often in isolated sites, and employers provided schools in the factory village. This became a common habit, and factory, colliery and ironworks schools were part of the pre-1872 mosaic. They suited employers because they allowed paternalist control, and could be used to meet the minimum educational standards for child workers imposed from 1833 by the factory and mine acts, whose enforcement in Scotland seems to have been reasonably effective (Bolin-Hort, 1991).

Contemporaries saw the demand for child labour as the chief threat to effective schooling, conflicting with Scottish rural customs which continued part-time education well into adolescence. Factory work, and the numerous types of casual work available to children in towns, cut off this extended education, and meant (for example) that children might leave school before learning to write. The factory legislation, which required 'half-time' schooling for child workers below a statutory age, can be seen as an attempt to compensate for this and restore the part-time tradition. So can the many evening courses in basic literacy which existed in towns and industrial villages, and, not least, the Sunday school movement, which began in the 1780s with factory children in mind. The earliest Sunday (or Sabbath) schools were run by voluntary societies rather than churches, and shunned by the Church of Scotland as politically suspect. But they soon became a central element in congregational activity, reached a high proportion of the working class, and only gradually switched from filling the gaps in secular education to a purely religious role (C.G. Brown, 1981–3).

If we turn from the provision of schools to the politics of education, religion again looms large, at a time when denominations and political parties were closely linked (W.H. Bain, 1978; I.G.C. Hutchison, 1986; Withrington, 1993; Anderson, 1995). A succession of parliamentary bills aiming at creating a 'national' system began in 1850, most of them sponsored by the Liberal Lord Advocate James Moncreiff. But his only legislative success was to remove direct control of the parish schools from the established church in 1861. The issue of control was at the heart of Moncreiff's difficulties: the Church of Scotland's educational role gave it an influence no longer justified by numbers alone, and it found allies in the landed class, determined to preserve the position of the heritors. Much of the political wrangling and obstruction centred on the issue of religious instruction in schools, and when the 1872 settlement was eventually achieved, by Moncreiff's successor James Young, it was only by allowing Catholic and Episcopalian schools to remain outside school board control; they received their grants direct from the state until 1918.

These controversies also embraced specifically Scottish grievances. The privy council grants were designed with English conditions in mind. They were modified for the Scottish religious situation, but there were periodic complaints that Scottish traditions, especially the widespread teaching of Latin and other higher subjects, were ignored. This issue came to a head in the Revised Code controversy of 1864, when Scottish objections were strong enough to postpone the application of new financial regulations, and to secure the appointment of the Argyll commission (Cruickshank, 1967; T. Wilson in Humes and Paterson, 1983). The commission endorsed Moncreiff's reform plans, and his last bill was presented, and defeated, in 1869. It has been argued that the Moncreiff bills, which tried to safeguard the parish schools as a distinctive part of the new national system, had general Scottish support and failed only because of the English majority at Westminster, while the 1872 Act was modelled on the English legislation of 1870 (Myers, 1972). The first part of this argument underestimates the religious and political opposition to the bills within Scotland. As for anglicization, the two acts did have many common features, but the Scottish reform went further by persuading all the presbyterian churches to transfer their schools to the boards, whereas in England school boards were only set up where church schools were lacking, and a powerful church sector survived in rivalry with them. This dual system caused much controversy, requiring further legislation in 1902 and 1944. In Scotland the 1872 settlement put a decisive end to politico-religious disputes, and (it can be argued) created the national, unified system called for since 1850 (Withrington, 1972; Anderson, 1995). Even so, the act left much Scottish opinion discontented, complaining about inadequate guarantees for higher subjects, the refusal of state aid for secondary schools, and lack of autonomy for the London-based SED (Scotland, 1972; Lenman and Stocks, 1972).

The period from 1872 to 1918, the era of the school boards, has attracted remarkably little archive-based research despite an abundance of records. There has been only one study of a major board, Glasgow, the scale of whose problems probably made it untypical (Roxburgh, 1971). One thing which is clear is that the secularization of education was a gradual process (C.G. Brown, 1987). In the early years religious issues dominated elections, and there was a heavy presence of clergymen. Parochialism and personal vendettas could paralyse the smaller boards (A. Bain, 1995), while in the cities the dominance of businessmen and other local notables left control in much the same hands as before 1872. But school board politics, including the growth of labour representation, need more research, as does the role of women, who could both vote for boards and become members (Anderson, 1995).

Larger urban boards could build a progressive reputation in areas of policy where they had discretion, but the core tasks – enforcing attendance, building and extending schools, delivering the elementary curriculum – were laid down in the SED's annual Code and enforced through its grants, which were as important to school board income as local rates. The SED's policies, though their public aspects are well-documented, also need more research. The Department acquired real autonomy in 1885 when it came under the new Secretary for Scotland, and was able to dominate and centralize policy more effectively than its English counterpart. Much was due to its powerful secretaries, Henry Craik (1885–1904) and John Struthers (1904–23). Both were creative as well as autocratic figures, although their conception of the social role of education ran on conventional class lines. But even the most powerful bureaucrat could not step beyond the limits of political control and Treasury rules. The system could be manipulated at the margins – Craik introduced free elementary education in 1890, slightly earlier than in England, and developed a policy on secondary schools which went well beyond the 1872 Act – but within the unitary state the scope for divergence from a British pattern was limited.

Scottish experiences are of special interest because of Scotland's very rapid industrialization and urbanization. An essentially rural system with a religious ethos, centred on the parish schools as both ideal and reality, had to be transformed for an urban, mass society. But the construction of state systems of elementary education was a general phenomenon of the age. It can be related to the rise of political democracy, marked in Britain by the Second Reform Act of 1867; to the evolution of the modern nation-state, in an age of industrial and military rivalry between the great powers, requiring both more highly educated workers and the inculcation of loyalty and citizenship into the masses; and to the general advance of secularization, transferring social functions from church to state under the guidance of the liberal bourgeoisie.

The statist teleology of conventional interpretations has, however, been challenged by West, extending to Scotland a market-based critique of the 1870 English Act. He argues that private enterprise was capable of meeting working-class needs, that the Scottish statistics show 'private' schools to be flourishing in the 1860s, and that almost all working-class children were educated without the need for compulsion. This argument fails to distinguish between the voluntary schools, which existed in symbiosis with the state, and genuine private schools, which were a small and declining sector (West, 1975; Anderson, 1983b; and cf. Mason, 1985, Anderson, 1985c). Yet West's work is a valuable reminder that mass education was fairly complete before schools became compulsory or free, and that much remains to be discovered about education in the cities and working-class attitudes towards it. And the voluntary sector itself, on whom the main burden lay for forty years, depended entirely on the willingness of church members to contribute their money and time. Growing reluctance to continue doing this, especially once large capital expenditure was needed to replace the first generation of schools and keep up with pedagogic evolution, was one reason why the 1872 Act was necessary.

State intervention, once established, had a tendency to expand. Compulsory schooling offered an obvious way of reaching working-class children, either to indoctrinate them with the political and moral qualities of good citizens, or to improve their physical welfare. Welfare policies were given a strong boost by the Boer War of 1899–1902, which revealed the poor physical state of the urban proletariat. This was the era of 'national efficiency', when Britain's military and industrial strength was held to depend on a healthy younger generation. The results included the systematic organization of physical education (I. Thomson, 1978; Anderson, 1985d), and the power given to school boards in 1908 to provide school meals and medical inspection. But here there was little difference between Scottish and English developments.

The growth of state intervention and the transition from social control through religion to the welfare role of the school form one perspective from which the nineteenth century can be viewed as a whole. Another is the relation of schooling to the development of class relations. The skilled workers and artisans of pre-industrial Scotland had often developed an interest in literature and ideas (Saunders, 1950), but there was little continuity between them and the new industrial proletariat. The new challenge was to teach the latter basic literacy, and the process was largely complete by 1872, through a mixture of spontaneous demand, market response, religious and charitable action by the middle classes, and indirect state aid. For most rural workers, and the respectable strata in the towns, there were state-aided schools with qualified teachers and a full curriculum. For the less fortunate – the urban poor, the inhabitants of the Western Isles, miners and factory workers whose education was curtailed by child labour – there were cheaper and inferior schools. The real achievement of the 1872 Act was to extend the same standard to all. It reflected the new political clout of working-class voters, and school boards gave at least the appearance of popular control. The schools which they built, along with other agencies of mass culture, became part of the everyday experience of the homogenized and mature working class which emerged in the later decades of the nineteenth century.

A third interpretative theme is the relation of schooling to gender. Female literacy had been much lower than male, often confined to reading, but in the nineteenth century both literacy and school attendance were virtually equalized (see Chapter 5), a change rooted in fundamental shifts of mentality which are still unexplored. Mixed schooling had been the rule in the parish schools, and the new schools founded in the nineteenth century were seldom strictly segregated (though Catholic schools were an exception). But at a time when middle-class views on the domestic role of women were strong, and when sewing was a compulsory girls' subject, there was a new demand for female teachers. Sometimes they acted as assistants in a mixed school, sometimes they conducted separate girls' schools. After 1872, most of these small schools were closed down, and school boards returned to the mixed tradition. Yet the separate girls' curriculum went on developing, with the addition of cookery and domestic economy. These female subjects were seen by their proponents not as a sign of inferiority, but as a speciality where women could make a distinctive contribution to social welfare, and a field of expertise in which women could find satisfying careers; colleges were founded in Edinburgh and Glasgow to train specialist teachers (Corr in Glasgow Women's Study Group, 1983, and in Fewell and Paterson, 1990; Begg, 1994). It has also been argued that this middle-class movement met resistance from working-class parents, partly because the long Scottish experience of mixed education, which had included the study of higher subjects like Latin and mathematics, created resistance to intellectual segregation (Moore, 1984, 1992).

Whether or not the separate girls' schools which expanded before 1872 accelerated female literacy, they certainly gave a more public role both to the upper and middle class women who founded and supervised them, and to female teachers, who otherwise had no chance of heading a school. The teaching profession and the training colleges provided new career opportunities and chances of social mobility, especially while women were still excluded from the universities. But the tradition of the graduate teacher meant that men dominated the profession for longer than in England, and Corr argues that women had a generally worse deal in Scotland (1990, 1995, and in

28

Humes and Paterson, 1983). They were not admitted until the 1870s to the professional association founded in 1847, the Educational Institute of Scotland, and while their numbers expanded greatly after 1872 they had to accept inferior salaries and promotion prospects. Even after 1918, when national salary scales were introduced, women were paid at lower rates and subject to the marriage bar (Adams, 1989).

A final long-term perspective is in terms of institutionalization and systematization. Informal modes of education, in the family or the community, were replaced by full-time schooling as the approved instrument of socialization (Sutherland, 1990). The compulsory day school prevailed over such alternatives as Sunday schools and evening courses, and a fixed period of schooling with a defined leaving age and a uniform curriculum (the 'three Rs') replaced the intermittent or seasonal attendance of rural society. Children were classified by age, class and gender, and subjected to mechanical and impersonal teaching methods. Historians of English education have recently stressed the resistance of working-class families to these trends, both before and after 1870, but no similar work has been done for Scotland.

What did worry Scots was that a systematic division between elementary and secondary education threatened to replace the looser structure which had developed since the Reformation, in which both burgh and parish schools served a broad spread of social classes and provided a path to the university by teaching Latin. Most of the new working-class schools, taught by men and women trained in professional techniques but without university degrees, were purely elementary. After 1872 it was feared that all board schools would be reduced to the same level, though in the event this threat was averted. There is a parallel here to the way in which a national system was dissolved by denominationalism, then reconstituted in 1872: popular and elite education seemed to draw apart in the nineteenth century, but moved together again in the twentieth.

CHAPTER 4

The Reshaping of Elite Education

The remodelling of secondary schools and universities in the nine-teenth century was as far-reaching as the development of mass education. Although this affected only a small segment of the population, the career demands of the expanding middle class and the need to keep open the channels of social mobility made reform a complex and sometimes controversial process. Elite education, precisely because it trained an elite which was still distinctive to Scotland, raised significant cultural issues, and the dominant inter-pretation of nineteenth-century university controversies remains that of Davie, who sees anglicization as the great motive power, and identifies rival patriotic and anglicizing parties among the reformers. Davie stresses the shift from a broad, generalized curriculum rooted in Scottish philosophical traditions to a narrower specialization typified by the single-subject honours degree. There was a parallel shift, Davie suggests, from the egalitarianism of the democratic intellect to a more class-based and socially exclusive education (Davie, 1964). Davie's immensely influential interpretation has been absorbed into many general books, and helped to establish the common view that breadth of curriculum is today the main distinguishing feature of Scottish education (McPherson, 1972). However, recent historians have criticized Davie's use of his sources, and given accounts of the university reform movement which stress the complexity of the explanatory factors involved (Anderson, 1983a; Withrington, 1992, and in Carter and Withrington, 1992).

The Scottish experience makes nonsense of the view, often found in anglocentric histories, that state interest in universities is a twentieth-century phenomenon. The Scottish universities engaged the attention of the state well before it intervened seriously in popular education, and occupied parliament intermittently for seventy years. There were commissions of inquiry in 1826 and 1876, and major acts of parliament in 1858 and 1889, which set up temporary executive commissions whose ordinances regulated the universities in precise and uniform detail. With minor exceptions in 1889, there were no university representatives on any of these commissions. This external intervention was in line with Scottish traditions of state visitation, which treated the universities as national and public institutions.

To bring them under closer control by public opinion was one aim of the reform movement which began in the 1820s, in a political climate hostile to closed corporations. It was not that the universities were stagnant – numbers were rising, and both Edinburgh University (Fraser, 1989) and Marischal College were completely rebuilt in this period – but rather that expansion and modernization came up against institutional constraints (Morrell, 1972–3). Reformers criticized the professoriate as a self-perpetuating clerical oligarchy, and identified various legal and organizational obstacles to efficiency: obsolete endowments, the control of Edinburgh University by the town council, squabbles between the professors at Glasgow, the continuing independence of the two colleges at Aberdeen. The Church of Scotland was powerful enough to block immediate reform, but the religious test for university professors was abolished in 1853, and the rest of the reform package came in the 1858 Act, which created University Courts with lay representatives to control appointments, and General Councils to give graduates (which meant in practice local professional elites) a say in university government (Horn, 1958–60).

The curriculum was thus only one issue, though an important one. The pressures for its reform included intellectual ones of which Germany was the principal source, such as the prestige of the neo-humanist classical ideal, the rise of laboratory-based natural science and scientific medicine, and a university model in which teaching was fused with research and scholarship. But they were also social. The strong nineteenth-century movement of professionalization made qualifications and examinations central to middle-class ambitions; meritocracy replaced patronage and hereditary privilege, and formal training began to take over from older modes of apprenticeship. Examples included the application of competitive examinations to the civil service, and the organization of medicine in 1858 as a state-regulated profession with graduate entry. Since Scottish parents wanted their sons to compete on equal terms, qualifications had to be assimilated to a British pattern. Within the universities themselves, reformers thought mainly in terms of academic and scholarly

31

standards, and wanted to raise the age of entry from 15 to 17 or 18, to introduce a strict entrance examination, and to restore formal graduation as the normal goal of university study. This in turn had implications for schools, requiring a more advanced secondary education, and threatening the direct link between parish school and university. Hence the controversies of the time: but it is misleading to see the reformers as any less patriotic, or concerned for the interests of Scottish students, than those who defended the older traditions of open and informal study.

The executive commission of 1858 laid down a coherent curriculum with a careful balance of linguistic, philosophical and mathematical content, introduced new subjects like English, encouraged graduation, and provided an honours system for those who wished it. But all arts students still had to go through a fixed range of seven or eight subjects. The 1889 commission went much further, allowing a choice of subjects within disciplinary groups, and introducing a bifurcation between four-year honours and three-year 'ordinary' degrees. With further changes in the 1900s, this was the Scottish arts curriculum familiar in the twentieth century. But one should not exaggerate the amount of specialization involved: students still had a common first and second year, and until well after the Second World War only a minority took honours degrees.

There are some flaws in Davie's concentration on the arts curriculum. One is that although his book is based on an implicit comparison with England, his English model of specialization is anachronistically modern. In the nineteenth century, Oxford and Cambridge were as concerned as the Scottish universities with a general, liberal education, though one based on classics and mathematics rather than philosophy, and the degree programme of London University, used by most English university colleges, was at least as multi-disciplinary as the Scottish one (Wright, 1979). Specialization developed later in both countries. Secondly, although the Scottish curriculum certainly embodied a distinctive ethos, it had not provided a standardized experience for the Scottish elite since the eighteenth century, when developments had encouraged flexibility and freedom of choice. The 1858 settlement reacted against this, but once graduation again become the norm, the uniform syllabus (which included compulsory Latin and Greek) cracked under the strain of vocational demands and pressure for more advanced teaching. In the 1860s the universities developed science degrees outside the arts framework, leading to separate science faculties after 1889. Another departure from the traditional mould was the foundation of University College at Dundee in 1883, preparing initially for London degrees, though in the 1890s it was affiliated to St Andrews (Southgate, 1982). Above all, there was medicine, which did not require an arts degree as a prerequisite, and which was transformed in the nineteenth century by the progress of medical science (Pennington, 1994). Numerous new chairs were founded, expensive buildings were constructed and equipped, and between 1860 and 1914 medical students generally formed 40–50% of the total at Edinburgh, 25–30% at Glasgow and Aberdeen (Anderson, 1983a, 348–56). The role of medicine in the universities – and of medical students in the corporate and athletic life which burgeoned in the late nineteenth century (Anderson, 1987b, 1988) – can hardly be overestimated.

Davie's book is at its best in its classic analysis of the philosophical core of the Scottish curriculum. By the early nineteenth century, the dominant school was the 'common sense' philosophy derived from Thomas Reid's reaction against Hume, which sought to reconcile rationalism and religious belief. Its psychological and epistemological concerns were narrower than those of the high Enlightenment, but still formed a powerful teaching tool in the hands of men like Dugald Stewart, professor at Edinburgh in 1785–1810 (Phillipson in Phillipson, 1983). To the regret of Davie and others (A. Thomson, 1985), this Scottish tradition did not renew itself in the nineteenth century, and gave way to more cosmopolitan trends like positivism and neo-Hegelianism, which usually arrived from the continent via England. By the end of the nineteenth century, most Scottish philosophy chairs were filled by neo-Hegelian idealists trained at Oxford, teaching a new ethos of citizenship and public service. But the dream that Scotland might one day recover a philosophical tradition of its own, to mark it off from England as Calvinism had done before the secularization of European thought, accounts for the lasting appeal of Davie's work to nationally-minded intellectuals, and the frequent reproduction of his ideas in polemical works which lack his subtlety of judgement.

The university entrance examination demanded by reformers eventually came in 1892, and corresponded to the Leaving Certificate for secondary schools, taken at 17, created by the SED in 1888. The history of university reform cannot be understood without looking also at the schools. Here the state was slower to act, because vigorous expansion was possible without any need for legislation. The process of amalgamating burgh schools to form new academies or high schools continued down to the 1860s. In the cities, they were supplemented by numerous private schools at all levels. A few 'proprietary' schools with salaried staffs were also founded, including Edinburgh Academy (1824) and Glasgow Academy (1846). But these were less common than in England, because burgh schools were better at adapting to middle-class needs than English grammar schools. In most towns the reformed burgh school dominated the scene, with the support of local elites. In some cases, as at St Andrews (Madras College, founded by the educationist Andrew Bell), Dollar or Fochabers, successful native sons provided large endowments, usually including free education for local children. Some endowments, notably the Dick bequest in the north-east (Cruickshank, 1965), sought to encourage higher education in parish schools, while in the cities the wealthy could immortalize their names by founding a residential 'hospital' giving free education to selected children. Some hospitals dated from before 1800 – George Heriot's at Edinburgh, George Watson's and the Merchant Maiden, run for boys and girls respectively by the Edinburgh Merchant Company, and Robert Gordon's at Aberdeen. But the nineteenth century saw new foundations such as John Watson's, Donaldson's and Daniel Stewart's at Edinburgh, and Morgan's in Dundee. The continuation of substantial educational endowments in the nineteenth century testifies to the profits being generated by economic expansion, to the place which education held in Scottish life, and to the spirit of local loyalty and self-reliance.

By the 1860s there was a growing movement for the systematic reorganization of secondary education, stimulated by the need for a more standardized and examination-oriented syllabus, by criticism of the hospital model as a wasteful use of resources, and by the deficiencies revealed in the Argyll commission's report on 'burgh and middle class schools'. Most Scottish opinion thought this an appropriate field for state action, but English politicians did not. The 1872 Act transferred the burgh schools to school boards, and the leading ones were designated as 'higher class' schools. But boards were forbidden to spend ratepayers' money on the latter, and there was no state finance for secondary education. Any new resources had to be found from the reform of existing endowments, and this became for a time the main instrument of change. A first act of 1869 was used by the Edinburgh Merchant Company to transform its hospitals into large day schools, and further legislation in 1878 and 1882 created

34

temporary commissions to put through individual reform schemes (Anderson, 1983a).

The 1882 commission, headed by Lord Balfour of Burleigh, carried out a thorough overhaul of urban endowments, applying the day-school model to most surviving hospitals. There was usually provision for scholarships from elementary schools, and the idea of transferring 'bright' children to secondary education around the age of 12 originates here. But endowment reform was controversial: it was accused of diverting funds from the poor to the middle classes, leaving only a narrow ladder of opportunity for the exceptionally talented. The case of George Heriot's, whose clientele had been the working-class elite of Edinburgh, was especially bitterly fought. These changes in the 1870s and 1880s created a long-lasting pattern of secondary education in Glasgow and Edinburgh, linked intimately with middle-class life and careers. Most private schools disappeared, leaving proprietary and endowed schools to share the market with the high schools run by the school boards, and subtle social differentiation was reinforced by the development of team games on the English model, especially rugby (Anderson, 1985d; Mangan and Loughlan, 1988).

The 1872 Act and the reform of endowments produced a category of 'higher class and endowed' schools which were fully secondary and met the demands of university reformers. Their development was strongly supported by Craik at the SED, and he was able to divert modest central funding in their direction. But this was not the only source of secondary education. The SED Code for elementary schools included grants for 'specific subjects' (including Latin and Greek) taught at higher levels, and these were used by school boards both to maintain higher teaching in former parish schools, and to develop quasi-secondary education in the towns. This was pushed furthest in the large cities, notably Glasgow, where 'higher grade' schools emerged in the 1880s which were secondary in all but name. The higher grade schools could give a chance to scholars transferred from elementary schools, but they were mainly designed to meet the needs of the expanding lower middle class, who wanted to go beyond elementary education but could not afford the older high schools and academies. The school boards inherited the wide social range of schools which had existed before 1872, and board schools were never used solely by the working class. As long as fees were charged, schools could reflect the social character of their district, and when fees were

35

abolished in 1890 school boards were allowed to keep them in higher grade schools (Roxburgh, 1971; Anderson, 1983a, 1995).

These changes were complicated and politically controversial. In the 1870s and 1880s two distinct conceptions were in conflict. The champions of true secondary education, including the SED, influential university professors, and the orthodox educational experts of both political parties, argued that to be effective it must be concentrated in a limited number of schools, properly financed through the fees paid by the middle class, but with a scholarship 'ladder' which talented elementary pupils might climb. Against them, radical Liberals, progressive school boards, and educational traditionalists led by the EIS set an ideal based on the parish schools: secondary education should be built organically on top of elementary, and higher subjects should be taught as widely as possible. The result, it has been argued (Anderson, 1983a, 1995), was a compromise. When a direct subsidy for secondary education was introduced in 1892, political pressure ensured that it was distributed widely through county committees, representing school boards and local authorities. The teaching of higher subjects in rural schools disappeared in all but remote districts, but the funds were used to support a network of secondary schools in every town of any size, instead of being concentrated as the SED preferred. Many of these schools were free, and the channels of mobility remained open. They had never been as wide as the idealizers of the parish school claimed – but this episode showed how the democratic myth could have a potent and creative political role. It was in 1894, after all, that the kailyard writer 'Ian Maclaren' launched the term 'lad o'pairts' into the world (Anderson, 1985b).

The development of women's education is a final theme linking schools and universities, though the latter have received more attention. In the early nineteenth century, most middle-class girls attended private schools, which left no records and seldom attracted comment in official inquiries. The movement towards a more academic education designed to put girls on the same intellectual level as boys, which started around 1850 in England, was slow to take hold in Scotland, perhaps because girls could already attend most burgh schools. The Argyll commission, unlike the simultaneous English Taunton commission, ignored the question. But change began in the late 1860s, though angled more to higher than to secondary education. 'Ladies' Educational Associations' were founded in the university towns, offering part-time courses in arts subjects, often given by sympathetic university professors, and these could lead to diplomas at degree level ratified by the universities (Moore, 1977–80, 1979–80, 1991). But the attempt in 1869 by Sophia Jex-Blake and others to gain direct entry to Edinburgh University as medical students failed, partly because of hostility from professors and students, partly because the courts decided that women could not be admitted without a change in the law. Thus while women's colleges were founded at Oxford and Cambridge, and women were admitted to the English civic universities, Scottish women had to wait until 1892, following the 1889 Act, to matriculate in the universities.

By that time, the secondary ground was well prepared. The reorganization of the Edinburgh Merchant Company schools in 1870 included two large modern girls' schools, and in Glasgow the reform of the Hutchesons' endowment in 1876 included a girls' grammar school. A number of proprietary schools for girls were also founded in the 1870s and 1880s, notably in Glasgow, and Glasgow and Aberdeen school boards eventually created their own girls' high schools. In these three cities, segregation remained the norm, and co-education arrived only with higher grade schools. But elsewhere all school boards continued the practice of mixed secondary schooling, which was not the case in England; one negative consequence was that the demand for graduate women teachers was limited, and even the girls' schools in the cities had male heads until the 1900s. Although one cannot say that Scotland took a pioneering role in the growth of girls' education, by 1900 middle-class parents had as good a choice of schools for daughters as for sons, and the curriculum, now oriented towards the Leaving Certificate, was essentially the same.

The number of women university students grew rapidly after 1900, and by 1914 they formed about 23% of the total (Anderson, 1983a, 357). But studies of university life show that their role was still restricted. Women were not fully admitted to the medical school at Edinburgh, and at Glasgow they were long taught separately in medicine, and even in arts subjects. As students, women had to develop their own forms of social life; they were obviously excluded from such strongholds of masculinity as rugby clubs and volunteer military corps, and found it difficult to break into student journalism or into the Students' Representative Councils which had developed since the 1880s (Hamilton, 1983; Anderson, 1988; Moore, 1991). Finally, although some new professional opportunities opened up for women graduates, such as social work, the range of available careers remained narrow (Kendall, 1991). The great majority of arts and science graduates went into teaching, and in medicine professional prejudice barred women from many posts (Alexander, 1987). The legal profession was still closed entirely to women, and the universities themselves hardly set an example: a few women became lecturers or assistants in the 1900s, but there was no Scottish woman professor before the Second World War. Thus the admission of women to universities was not a definitive removal of inequalities, but more an adjustment, though a significant one, in the distribution of gender roles.

It was also part of the systematization and professionalization of elite education. Women's education shows especially clearly the transition from informal to highly structured modes of education, which is characteristic equally of the reform of the university curriculum and of the remodelling of the burgh and endowed schools into a homogeneous secondary system. This achievement was in many ways an impressive one. Intellectual standards were raised, and the middle-class demand for qualifications allowing Scots to compete for jobs on a British basis was well satisfied. But systematization also meant accentuating the differences between elite and popular education. At the end of the nineteenth century, as in other European countries, elementary and secondary education were two sectors with some narrow bridges between them, not successive stages in an integrated system.

CHAPTER 5

Measuring Outcomes

Generalizations about school attendance, social mobility, or the democratic nature of Scottish education are given more weight if they can be supported statistically, an approach which also allows cross-national comparisons. The most basic indications of educational progress are literacy and school enrolments, and these figures underline the way in which 1872 marked the consolidation rather than the introduction of universal education. Table 1 shows the progress of literacy after marriage signatures were first recorded in 1855.

Table 1. Literacy of Brides and Bridegrooms, 1855–1900 (%)

	Men	Women
1855	89	77
1860	90	78
1865	89	78
1870	90	80
1875	91	83
1880	92	85
1885	94	89
1890	96	93
1895	97	95
1900	98	97

Source: Anderson, 1995, 305.

Since marriage took place ten or fifteen years after leaving school, the immediate pre-1872 situation is reflected in the figures for 1885; the narrowing of the gap between men and women had been the chief achievement since 1850. But national percentages conceal the fact

39

that most counties were almost wholly literate before 1872, the main exceptions being the western highlands and the Glasgow region (Anderson, 1995, 306–7). Moreover, 1855 is late in the process, and we do not know whether there had been steady improvement since the period studied by Houston, or more complex fluctuations. Further research on this key period of industrialization and urbanization, building on the pioneering work of Webb (1954), is badly needed.

The same may be said of school attendance. The first attempt to count the pupils in Scottish schools was a parliamentary return for 1818, an exercise which had many deficiencies (see Withrington, 1988b). This and later estimates are summarized in Table 2. The figures were compiled in different ways and give a misleading impression of precision: the 1864 total, for example, comes from the Argyll commission, which relied on heroic extrapolation to fill the gaps in its statistical work. But the overall story of growth outpacing general demographic expansion is clear. The places/population ratio in the final column is a crude calculation often used for international comparisons, in which Scotland usually came out among the leaders. In 1911, after forty years of compulsion, there were to be 178 pupils in state elementary schools per thousand population (Anderson, 1995, 233). The rate at which children were brought into school before 1872 is therefore impressive, though the lack of reliable figures before 1833 makes it difficult to say just when this silent revolution began.

Table 2. School Attendance, 1818–1873

Year	Pupils	Per 1000 population
1818	176,525	84
1833–4	236,325	100
1851	310,442	108
1864	418,367	137
1873	515,353	153

Source: Anderson, 1995, 103.

For more precision, we can turn to the 1871 and later censuses, which give the percentage of children attending school (as claimed by parents, therefore probably on the optimistic side) for each annual age-group and for each parish or registration district in Scotland. This is a remarkable source, which, like the early parliamentary returns and the registrar-general's literacy figures, has unrealized potential for the computer-based analysis of regional and local variations. The general attendance figures for Scotland for 1871–1901 are shown in Table 3. This illustrates the impact of compulsory education, which was initially from the fifth to the thirteenth birthday (age-groups 5 to 12 in the table), and after 1883 from 5 to 14 (age-groups 5 to 13), though until 1901 many exemptions were allowed. Attendance was already high in 1871, but there were still gaps to be filled, and compulsion had made a significant difference by 1881. Another point of interest is that attendance as young as five had not been a general habit, and parents remained reluctant for some years to conform with the new rule.

Table 3. School Attendance as Percentage of Age-Group, 1871–1901

Age	1871 B	1871 G	1881 B	1881 G	1891 B	1891 G	1901 B	1901 G
3	2	2	3	3	2	2	1	1
4	9	9	12	11	13	12	10	10
5	52	48	51	48	58	56	64	62
6	76	73	82	80	88	87	95	95
7	87	84	93	91	95	94	100	99
8	91	89	95	94	96	96	100	100
9	92	89	96	95	97	97	100	100
10	90	88	96	95	96	96	100	100
11	84	83	95	94	95	95	100	99
12	70	72	90	90	86	87	97	98
13	41	40	65	67	59	63	82	85
14	23	22	32	34	30	32	33	37

Source: Anderson, 1995, 234.

The figures for 1871 help to answer a question debated by both contemporaries and historians: how many children were escaping schooling altogether on the eve of 1872? The Argyll commission gave an ambiguous answer, because, as was frequent at the time, it related pupils within a specified age range to the total size of the age-group, without data for specific annual cohorts. This produced a 'deficiency'

41

percentage whose significance really depended on the average length of schooling, but which was often taken to indicate a mass of 'unschooled' children (see West, 1975). Using the age-group 5 to 13, Argyll calculated that the deficiency was 18% for Scotland as a whole, and about a third for Glasgow. The historian James Scotland, perhaps misreading this, said that 'a third of Scottish children in the sixties did not attend any school', and this quite unjustified statement has found its way into several general histories (Scotland, 1969, vol. 1, 359; cf. Anderson, 1995, 105–7). In fact the 1871 census shows that for the 5–13 age-group the overall deficiency was 20% for boys and 22% for girls, which is not so far from the Argyll estimate. But the average attendance was probably about four years, and at the peak ages between eight and ten it reached 90–92% for boys and 88–89% for girls. Since the theoretical maximum of 100% was difficult to achieve, it seems likely that fewer than 10% were escaping school attendance of some kind, though its quality was another matter.

Table 4. School Attendance by Age, 1871

		% attending at age										
		5	6	7	8	9	10	11	12	13	14	5–12
Roxburgh	B	55	85	94	97	97	98	93	87	53	29	88
	G	47	75	92	95	94	97	93	83	44	25	85
Fife	B	69	88	93	96	96	96	90	75	44	25	88
	G	64	88	93	95	94	92	86	72	32	16	85
Ross & Cromarty	B	45	61	76	85	86	87	88	87	71	42	77
	G	43	60	73	77	84	83	84	79	61	36	73
Glasgow	B	34	62	79	86	88	85	77	60	28	12	71
	G	30	62	74	85	84	84	79	67	31	15	70
Edinburgh	B	62	86	93	94	96	94	89	78	49	28	86
	G	59	82	91	94	94	94	91	83	53	30	86
Dundee	B	66	80	84	88	86	81	72	53	26	13	77
	G	62	77	82	85	83	75	67	48	17	8	73
Coatbridge	B	45	67	80	86	84	84	65	45	19	9	69
	G	42	66	84	85	86	85	75	65	38	23	72

Source: Anderson, 1995, 123–5, 135–6.

Low attendance was concentrated in black spots, which the 1871 figures also reveal. Table 4 gives a small selection for certain counties and towns. Roxburghshire is an example of the high levels achieved in many lowland counties; few here escaped schooling, and the similar figures for Fife show that industrialization as such was not a bar to high attendance. Nor was urbanization, as Edinburgh shows – and the figures for Aberdeen and Inverness were even higher. For Glasgow, on the other hand, attendance levels suggest that at least 10% of boys and 15% of girls were going unschooled. Similar figures were characteristic of the west of Scotland, though the presence of Irish Catholics, as also in Dundee, provides part of the explanation (Mason, 1985).

Three other points emerge from Table 4. First, Ross and Cromarty shows the low attendance in parts of the highlands, though this was concentrated in the west of the county. It also shows a pattern of prolonged education which was characteristic of all the highland counties: about 40% of children were still at school at 14. The older customs of intermittent attendance survived here when they were disappearing in the lowlands. The second point is the impact of child labour. The pattern in Dundee was typical of textile towns, where the factory work was for girls, while Coatbridge was a coal and iron centre, where it was the boys who left early. In several mining counties, girls' overall attendance was slightly higher than boys', reversing the usual pattern (Anderson, 1983b, 1995). These variations help to explain why compulsory education was thought necessary. The third point is a more general one: there is a close correlation between the geographical patterns of literacy and of school attendance, which suggests both that the data correspond to some underlying reality, and that in Scotland literacy was predominantly a school-based phenomenon.

Once school attendance becomes compulsory and basic literacy universal, the statistics of elementary education lose much of their interest for the social historian. Attention switches instead to the length of schooling and the extent of participation in secondary and higher education, for which a different type of source is available: breakdowns of the social origins of students – and also their birthplaces, ages and prior education – derived either from surveys of the time, or through analysis of matriculation records.

For secondary schools, material of this kind exists only for 1866. It shows that the old burgh schools were used by the middle class in a broad sense, from professional families at the top to small shop-keepers and clerks at the bottom, but hardly at all by the working class, for whom the fees were an insuperable barrier: there were few bursaries in burgh schools (Anderson, 1983a, 138–40). In smaller towns, the burgh schools had a real community function. In the cities, they were used by the kind of professional and business families who might have used public schools in England, though the topmost elite were already sending their sons south, or using the more exclusive schools like Edinburgh Academy. After 1872, social recruitment was widened by the growth of scholarship schemes and the lowering or abolition of fees, but serving the middle class remained the main function of the urban secondary school (Anderson, 1985d).

Table 5. Socio-Occupational Origins of University Students (%)

	1866			1910			
	Edinburgh	Glasgow	Aberdeen	Glasgow M	W	Aberdeen M	W
Professional	35	30	29	26	27	20	24
Commercial/industrial	15	20	9	25	27	13	14
Agricultural	13	13	29	3	7	13	20
Intermediate	8	6	7	20	19	16	12
Working class	25	24	17	24	18	14	15

Source: Anderson, 1983a, 150–1, 310–15.

For universities, the data are more abundant, and Table 5 compares the socio-occupational backgrounds of students in the 1860s (from the Argyll report) and in 1910 (from matriculation records). The grouping of occupations is a broad one: most 'agricultural' parents were farmers, not crofters or labourers; most 'intermediate' ones were shopkeepers or clerks; in the 'working class' group, artisans and skilled workers far outnumbered factory workers, miners, or the unskilled. Nevertheless, the figures do show the genuinely popular character of the Scottish universities. About half the students came from the two upper or 'bourgeois' groups, half from the three lower ones, where the fathers themselves were unlikely to have had a university or even secondary education. The lads of parts existed, but they were above all the children of professional men, small businessmen, farmers, white-collar workers, and artisans. It was from this group – drawn perhaps more from the Scotland of farms and small towns than from the industrial cities – that the elite was renewed. The 'intermediate' group were the main gainers by 1910, while within the middle class the business element had gained on the professional; the proportion of working-class students stayed much the same. It seems therefore that the anglicization of the curriculum did not lead to social restriction, and that the systematic development of secondary education opened up new opportunities, though for the middle as much as the working class. Women students came from similar backgrounds to men, but were rather more likely to come from middle-class or farming families.

The matriculation records at Aberdeen and Glasgow are now being computerized, and these are already the best-documented universities. The Glasgow figures given above are broadly confirmed by an independent sampling (Robertson, 1990), and can be related both backwards to Mathew's work (1966) and forwards to data from the 1930s and the 1960s (McDonald, 1967). The social character of the university changed remarkably little over the years, and at both middle-class and working-class levels it reflected the commercial and industrial activities of the city. At Aberdeen, whose character was similarly marked by its rural hinterland, the interest of the data lies in the potential for linking students' origins with their eventual occupations. They show, for example, that students of rural or working-class origin tended to become ministers or schoolteachers, rather than moving into the more prestigious professions. At Aberdeen, about half of the graduates had to leave Scotland to find posts, elsewhere in Britain or overseas, and this may well have been typical of the Scottish universities (Mackay, 1969; Mercer and Forsyth, 1975; Anderson, 1988; Hargreaves, 1994).

This picture of wide social recruitment needs to be set against the fact that the universities enrolled a very small proportion of the population, as shown in Table 6. The right-hand column relates student places to the total Scottish population. The Argyll report included some often-cited international comparisons based on such figures, and claimed that Scotland was a leader in both secondary and university education. For secondary schools, this is misleading (Anderson, 1985a), and Table 7 shows the census figures for school attendance up to age 17. This suggests that no more than 4% of the age-group completed secondary education, which is in line with

European norms, but no better. The significant change between 1871 and 1911 was in the quality of secondary schools, especially for girls, rather than in attendance.

Table 6. University Enrolments

Year	No. of students			Per 1000 population	
	Men	Women	Total	Men	Total
1800	c.3,000			1.9	
1826	c.4,250			1.8	
1861	3,399			1.1	
1871	3,984			1.2	
1881	6,595			1.8	
1891	6,604			1.6	
1901	5,346	908	6,254	1.2	1.4
1911	5,924	1,846	7,770	1.2	1.6
1921	8,247	3,162	11,409	1.7	2.3
1931	7,674	3,398	11,072	1.6	2.3
1951	11,149	3,862	15,011	2.2	3.0
1961	14,029	5,404	19,433	2.7	3.8

Source: Anderson, 1985a, 467.

Table 7. School Attendance in Higher Age-Groups, 1871–1911 (%)

Age	1871		1901		1911	
	B	G	B	G	B	G
14	23	22	33	37	39	38
15	13	13	12	16	13	13
16	7	7	5	8	7	9
17	4	4	2	4	4	6

Source: Anderson, 1995, 235.

It is less easy to calculate the participation ratio for universities, but they may have been attended by as many as 2% of the relevant male age-group in the nineteenth century, which was very high by international standards (Anderson, 1983a, 1985a, 1995). But while

46

university education expanded in other countries, Scotland's pre-cocious development meant a lack of long-term change in its social reach. Student numbers fluctuated, but hardly outpaced the general population; much of the twentieth-century growth was due to the admission of women, and although there was a boost in numbers after 1918 this only returned to the participation ratios of the 1880s. In secondary education, on the other hand, there was real change between the wars, with numbers more than doubling: in round figures, from 40,000 in 1913 to 90,000 in 1939, while Leaving Certificates awarded rose from about 1700 to over 4000 (Anderson, 1985a, 474–6). This was due partly to democratization, partly perhaps to pupils staying on till 17 who would formerly have left at 15.

For until the twentieth century the percentage staying at school beyond 15 or entering universities fell far short of the 'middle class' element in the population – by one estimate about a fifth even in the mid-nineteenth century (Morgan and Trainor, in Fraser and Morris, 1990). For most industrial or commercial careers, formal qualifications were not needed, and there was pressure to start work early; this pattern seems to be confirmed by studies of the education of businessmen (Anderson, 1991; Slaven and Kim, 1994), and explains why girls might stay on rather longer. University education and the extended school preparation needed for it were associated chiefly with the 'learned' professions. The fact that universities had only a limited appeal to the middle class left space for the student ranks to be socially mixed, but the working-class students themselves were a tiny minority of their class. In the nineteenth century, the middle classes enjoyed a first educational revolution in the quality and organization of their schooling: in the late twentieth century, there was to be a second revolution as the middle-class leaving age rose (always keeping a few years ahead of the working-class one) and university education became the norm. In both cases, the classes benefited almost as much as the masses from the active intervention of the state.

CHAPTER 6

The Twentieth Century

In the preceding chapters it has been possible to combine a discussion of recent interpretations with a reasonably comprehensive, if compressed, history of educational developments. For the twentieth century this is difficult: research has so far sunk only a few shafts into a complex field, and it seems best to concentrate on these. Two useful general surveys are available (Smout, 1986; McPherson, 1992), but the inter-war years are less well covered than those since 1945, where sociologists and political scientists have made an important (and historically well-informed) contribution to the study of educational policy (Gray, McPherson and Raffe, 1983; McPherson and Raab, 1988).

The central story is common to Scotland and England: the acceleration of social reform by two world wars; the acceptance by governments (from Asquith's Liberals onwards) of equality of opportunity as a formal goal; the raising of the school leaving age from 14 in 1901 to 15 in 1947 and 16 in 1973; the move from elite secondary schooling to 'secondary education for all', at first with selection leading to different types of school, later in the comprehensive schools introduced by a Labour government in 1965; and a huge expansion since the Second World War of examination qualifications and places in higher and further education. The formation of an integrated school system with successive primary and secondary stages is a central theme which directs special attention to SED policies. But something must first be said about the changing administrative framework.

School boards were abolished in England and Wales in 1902, but lasted in Scotland until 1918, and were then replaced by directly elected county and city education authorities until 1929, when education was transferred to the all-purpose local authorities, on the vagaries of whose funding and reorganization it was thereafter dependent. There is only one study of an *ad hoc* authority, Dunbartonshire

(A. Roberts in Bone, 1967), from which it appears that their initiative, especially in developing post-primary education, was severely limited by financial constraints. These authorities still contained many ministers of religion, and in the West of Scotland both Catholics and Labour were major electoral forces.

The 1918 Education Act is best remembered for the religious settlement which transferred Roman Catholic and Episcopalian schools, which had received revenue but not capital grants from the state since 1872, to the education authorities, with safeguards for the schools' religious character. While Episcopalian schools dwindled, the division between non-denominational and Catholic state schools became entrenched, and often produced sectarian friction. The 1918 settlement had been foreshadowed in pre-war negotiations, but the Catholic hierarchy was divided on its advantages, and tried for a time to retain some control by continuing to finance new building, though this proved too expensive to sustain (Kenneth, 1968; Treble, 1978, 1980; Darragh, 1990). Expansion was to be particularly significant in the secondary field, where poverty and the working-class nature of the Catholic community had inhibited development before 1918 (Fitzpatrick, 1986).

The 1918 Act proved less of a landmark in democratization than contemporaries hoped, partly because financial crisis postponed indefinitely the proposed raising of the leaving age to 15, partly because of the conservatism of the SED. The Department had grappled since the turn of the century with the problem of coordinating different levels of education, given new urgency by the takeover in 1898 of the Scottish work of the Science and Art Department, which had funded evening classes and technical education since the 1850s, and by the 1901 Education Act which abolished the right of children to leave early once they had mastered the basic skills. Some exemptions were still allowed, but 14 was now the true leaving age for most pupils, and new offerings had to be devised for those who stayed on. The SED's policy was to distinguish between secondary education proper, to which promising pupils should transfer at 12, and advanced elementary education for those leaving at 14 or 15, to be given in 'supplementary courses' with a distinctively vocational character. This policy, formalized in 1903, was linked with national efficiency thinking: the selection of able children, and a functional approach to matching education to intellectual aptitudes, were seen as the scientific way of exploiting the nation's human resources, reinforced between the wars by the development of intelligence testing.

49

The dualist policy met criticism even in the 1900s for putting an end to the parish school tradition, though in practice the wide availability of secondary schooling and bursaries made transfer out of elementary schools fairly extensive (Anderson, 1983a, 1995). The 1918 Act proclaimed the principle of free secondary education (putting Scotland well ahead of England), and there were wide hopes that the barriers would be broken down, but these were disappointed when the SED issued its controversial Circular 44 in 1921, followed by new regulations in 1923 which reasserted the existing policy. The supplementary courses were replaced by 'advanced divisions', but these were still denied secondary status, and most gave two-year rather than three-year courses (Paterson in Humes and Paterson, 1983; Stocks, 1995). This policy prevailed until the Education Act of 1936, which envisaged raising the leaving age to 15 in 1939. The outbreak of war postponed this, but SED policy in the 1940s was to reclassify all post-primary education in either senior (five-year) or junior (three-year) secondary courses. Secondary education for all, at least in nomenclature, was thus achieved.

In England, the gradual integration of elementary and secondary education was charted in major official reports – Hadow in 1926, Spens in 1938, Norwood in 1943. There was no equivalent in Scotland, but there was a similar process of change, and the realities in the 1920s and 1930s were more flexible than the theory (McPherson, 1992). Most authorities moved towards a 'clean cut' at the age of 12, and concentrated their advanced divisions in 'central' schools, the basis of the later junior secondaries. In smaller towns, though the courses remained distinct, secondary and advanced education were often given together in socially comprehensive 'omnibus' schools. Parents themselves resisted narrow vocationalism, and pushed their children into academic schools even if they had no intention of completing a secondary course. Yet the general picture was still of social segregation.

If the First World War raised hopes that were disappointed, the Second was more important for fuelling a long-term explosion of aspirations than for its immediate legislative effects. The 1944 Act for England and Wales is seen as a milestone of democratic reconstruction, but the Scottish equivalent in 1945 was only a consolidating measure. Lloyd's studies of policy-making during the war (1983, 1984, 1992a, 1992b) show that the SED had little taste for radical change, despite the proddings of the Labour Secretary of

State, Tom Johnston. Johnston tried to bypass the SED by reinvigorating the Advisory Council on Education (a body dating from 1918). Its report on secondary education in 1947 was a notably idealistic document, which restated the Scottish democratic ethos, but had little direct impact (Northcroft, 1992). By the 1960s the system of senior and junior secondary schools seemed well established, and the SED's priority was still to defend the academic, university-oriented tradition. McPherson has argued that it was the introduction of the 'O grade' examination in 1962 which made the pressure for change irresistible, by encouraging much greater numbers to stay on (McPherson and Raab, 1988; McPherson, 1992).

The move to comprehensive education, though essentially an outcome of British politics, was eased by the rhetoric of 1947 and the experience of omnibus schools, and in Scotland it has been regarded as a success; there has been little demand for its reversal, or nostalgia for the selective past, a divergence from English experiences for which history must provide part of the explanation (Gray, McPherson and Raffe, 1983; McPherson and Willms, 1986). But self-congratulatory amnesia has glossed over the dissent and sharp local conflicts which accompanied the change. The 1918 Act had allowed local authorities to keep some fee-paying schools, and the SED continued to give direct grants to endowed schools. Thus the existing pattern of middle-class schooling in the cities, especially Edinburgh and Glasgow, had survived (Highet, 1969). Comprehensive reorganization disrupted this, and the withdrawal of direct grants forced some leading schools once considered part of the public system to become independent, though being predominantly day schools they remained closer to the community and to the public educational ethos than their English counterparts.

Underlying these changes was a long-term growth of demand with demographic, social and economic roots, already apparent at secondary level before the 1939–45 war, and pushing on into higher education after it; Scottish participation ratios in both sectors have generally been ahead of English ones. But little has been written about university history after 1919, when the Scottish universities came under the control of the new University Grants Committee. Research on Aberdeen shows that even in its early days the UGC took a more directive role than is often supposed, and that after 1945 it imposed growth on a strongly regional and rather conservative institution (Hargreaves and Forbes, 1989; Hutchison, 1993). Scotland shared in the expansion associated with (but actually preceding) the Robbins report of 1963, which included a new foundation at Stirling, the separation of Dundee from St Andrews, and the creation out of technical colleges of Strathclyde and Heriot-Watt universities. Degree-level work also expanded in technical colleges and colleges of education, and in the 1990s there was a second wave of promotion to university status.

One result has been a welcome interest in the history of institutions other than the ancient universities (Begg, 1994; Ferguson, 1995; Butt, 1996; Harrison and Marker, 1996). The history of technical and other post-school education has previously been neglected, though it has been an important strand in policy. In the nineteenth century its development was haphazard, taking the form mainly of evening classes; many towns had art schools and technical colleges, but their prosperity depended on local initiatives. From around 1900 the SED had a systematic but selective policy for technical and 'continuation' education, on the one hand building up a handful of vocational 'central institutions' in the cities, on the other encouraging part-time continuation classes for adolescents, following on from elementary education and seeking to fill its deficiencies. The 1908 Education Act allowed school boards to experiment with compulsory continuation classes, and the 1918 Act intended to make them universal, but this was never implemented. The promotion of technical or adult education was not a high priority between the wars, and it was only after 1945 that a broader concept of further education was developed, and embodied in a network of local colleges. More research on technical education and its local links with industry and employers might give a Scottish dimension to the current debate on how far education contributed to Britain's economic difficulties in the twentieth century. So far this has been approached only at the university level: universities seem to have been reasonably responsive to local needs, in both teaching and research, but industrial and commercial employers were slow to value formal qualifications, and the demand for scientifically and technically trained graduates was limited (Sanderson, 1972; Robertson, 1984).

Two final issues have attracted recent debate: the alleged conservatism of Scottish education, and the significance of the democratic myth. Reacting against popular views of Scotland as educationally progressive, students of policy-making have stressed the conservatism of the educational establishment. The SED certainly lost the creative dynamism of Craik and Struthers under their successors, and McPherson uses oral interviews to argue that its officials and inspectorate were drawn disproportionately from the small-town milieu of the classic lad of parts (the 'Kirriemuir career'), making them strong defenders of the elitist version of Scottish meritocracy, but obstructing their grasp of the problems of working-class education, especially as they arose in the West (McPherson in Humes and Paterson, 1983; McPherson and Raab, 1988; cf. Humes, 1986). Davie, in a wide-ranging discussion of Scottish culture between the wars, accused the SED of imposing examination-oriented specialization on the universities (Davie, 1986). More generally, it has been observed that Scotland seldom led the way in progressive pedagogy (Osborne, 1966), and radical educationists like A.S. Neill in the 1920s or R.F. Mackenzie in the 1960s were prophets without honour in their own country. But against this, Lindsay Paterson (1996) has argued that progress was real, and that the Scottish 'policy community' had its progressive elements, including the Advisory Council, the EIS (at times), academic educationists, and bodies like the Scottish Council for Research in Education, founded in 1928.

A broader critique comes from Smout (1986, following Hamish Paterson in Humes and Paterson, 1983), who argues that careful attention to the elite and to opportunity for individuals was not matched in the education of the bulk of the population, which was always mediocre, and instilled conformist and socially limited outlooks. It is difficult to test this charge without more direct evidence, for little historical work has been done on twentieth-century primary education. One study in oral history, looking at childhood in rural Scotland, does seem to confirm that most education had very limited perspectives even after the leaving age was raised to 14, and that few could consider staying on (Jamieson in Glasgow Women's Studies Group, 1983; Jamieson in Fewell and Paterson, 1990; Jamieson and Toynbee, 1992).

This brings us back to the myth of the lad of parts, which has come under scrutiny both from historians (Anderson, 1983a, 1985b; Harvie, 1991) and from sociologists (McPherson, 1973; McPherson in Humes and Paterson, 1983; McCrone, 1992). This reflects a new interest in questions of national identity and self-image, made topical by the revival of Scottish political and cultural nationalism. Most observers agree that the myth of the lad of parts corresponds to some underlying reality, albeit idealized. It expressed a nineteenth-century ideal of meritocracy, which did allow for individual social mobility, yet also legitimized the reproduction through schooling of the inequalities of industrial society; even when meritocratic concepts challenged class barriers, they hardly acknowledged those of gender (Corr in Fraser and Morris, 1990). But it is striking that analysts of post-1945 policy have seen this myth playing a vital part in moulding events, just as it did in the nineteenth century (Gray, McPherson and Raffe, 1983; McPherson and Raab, 1988). It is not entirely fanciful to see in widespread acceptance of comprehensive schooling, in adherence to the ideal of a single, national system of education under public control, or in the belief that the power of the democratic state should counteract inequalities of wealth and social advantage, the living influence of four centuries of history.

SELECT BIBLIOGRAPHY

There are fuller bibliographies for the nineteenth century in Anderson (1983a, 1995). For original research, Craigie (1970, 1974) should be the starting-point. There are annual lists of new books and articles in *Scottish Historical Review* and *Scottish Economic and Social History*.

C. Adams, 'Women in teaching between the wars', *Scottish Educational Review* 21 (1989).

W. Alexander, *First Ladies of Medicine: the Origins, Education and Destination of Early Women Medical Graduates of Glasgow University* (Glasgow, 1987).

R.D. Anderson, *Education and Opportunity in Victorian Scotland: Schools and Universities* (Oxford, 1983a).

R.D. Anderson, 'Education and the state in nineteenth-century Scotland', *Economic History Review* 2nd series 36 (1983b).

R.D. Anderson, 'Education and society in modern Scotland: a comparative perspective', *History of Education Quarterly* 25 (1985a).

R.D. Anderson, 'In search of the "lad of parts": the mythical history of Scottish education', *History Workshop* 19 (1985b).

R.D. Anderson, 'School attendance in nineteenth-century Scotland: a reply', *Economic History Review* 2nd series 38 (1985c).

R.D. Anderson, 'Secondary schools and Scottish society in the nineteenth century', *Past and Present* 109 (1985d).

R.D. Anderson, 'Scottish university professors, 1800–1939: profile of an elite', *Scottish Economic and Social History* 7 (1987a).

R.D. Anderson, 'Sport in the Scottish universities, 1860–1939', *International Journal of the History of Sport* 4 (1987b).

R.D. Anderson, *The Student Community at Aberdeen, 1860–1939* (Aberdeen, 1988).

R.D. Anderson, 'Universities and elites in modern Britain', *History of Universities* 10 (1991).

R.D. Anderson, *Universities and Elites in Britain since 1800* (London, 1992).

R.D. Anderson, *Education and the Scottish People, 1750–1918* (Oxford, 1995).

A. Bain, *Education in Stirlingshire from the Reformation to the Act of 1872* (London, 1965).

A. Bain, *Patterns of Error: the Teacher and External Authority in Central Scotland, 1581–1861* (Edinburgh, 1989).

A. Bain, 'The first school board of Tulliallan, 1873–6: uneasy transition from Church to State', *Forth Naturalist and Historian* 18 (1995).

W.H. Bain, ' "Attacking the citadel": James Moncreiff's proposals to reform Scottish education, 1851–69', *Scottish Educational Review* 10 (1978).

J. Bannerman, 'Literacy in the Highlands', in I.B. Cowan and D. Shaw, eds., *The Renaissance and Reformation in Scotland: Essays in Honour of Gordon Donaldson* (Edinburgh, 1983).

J.M. Beale, *A History of the Burgh and Parochial Schools of Fife* (n.p., 1983).

R. Begg, *The Excellent Women: the Origins and History of Queen Margaret College* (Edinburgh, 1994).

P. Bolin-Hort, 'A decided failure? The enforcement of the early Factory Acts in the Glasgow district, 1834–1870', *Journal of the Scottish Labour History Society* 26 (1991).

T.R. Bone, *School Inspection in Scotland, 1840–1966* (London, 1968).

T.R. Bone, ed., *Studies in the History of Scottish Education, 1872–1939* (London, 1967).

W. Boyd, *Education in Ayrshire through Seven Centuries* (London, 1961).

C.G. Brown, 'The Sunday-school movement in Scotland, 1780–1914', *Scottish Church History Society Records* 21 (1981–3).

C.G. Brown, *The Social History of Religion in Scotland since 1730* (London, 1987).

S.J. Brown, 'The Disruption and urban poverty: Thomas Chalmers and the West Port operation in Edinburgh, 1844–47', *Scottish Church History Society Records* 20 (1978–80).

S.J. Brown, *Thomas Chalmers and the Godly Commonwealth* (Oxford, 1982).

J. Butt, *John Anderson's Legacy: the University of Strathclyde and its Antecedents, 1796–1996* (East Linton, 1996).

J.W. Cairns, 'The origins of the Glasgow law school: the professors of civil law 1741–61', in P. Birks, ed., *The Life of the Law: Proceedings of the Tenth British Legal History Conference. Oxford 1991* (London, 1993a).

J.W. Cairns, 'William Crosse, Regius Professor of Civil Law in the University of Glasgow, 1746–1749: a failure of enlightened patronage', *History of Universities* 12 (1993b).

J.W. Cairns, 'The law, the advocates and the universities in late sixteenth-century Scotland', *Scottish Historical Review* 73 (1994).

J.W. Cairns, 'Lawyers, law professors, and localities: the universities of Aberdeen, 1680–1750', *Northern Ireland Legal Quarterly* 46 (1995).

C. Camic, 'Experience and ideas: education for universalism in eighteenth-century Scotland', *Comparative Studies in Society and History* 25 (1983a).

C. Camic, *Experience and Enlightenment: Socialization for Cultural Change in Eighteenth-Century Scotland* (Edinburgh, 1983b).

R.H. Campbell and A. Skinner, eds., *The Origins and Nature of the Scottish Enlightenment* (Edinburgh, 1982).

R.G. Cant, 'The Scottish universities and Scottish society in the eighteenth century', *Studies on Voltaire and the Eighteenth Century* 58 (1967).

R.G. Cant, *The University of St Andrews: a Short History* (new ed., Edinburgh, 1970).

J.J. Carter and C.A. McLaren, *Crown and Gown: an Illustrated History of the University of Aberdeen, 1495–1995* (Aberdeen, 1994).

J.J. Carter and D. Withrington, eds., *Scottish Universities: Distinctiveness and Diversity* (Edinburgh, 1992).

J.J. Carter and J.H. Pittock, eds., *Aberdeen and the Enlightenment* (Aberdeen, 1987).

D. Chambers, 'The Church of Scotland's Highlands and Islands education scheme, 1824–1843', *Journal of Educational Administration and History* 7 (1975).

A.C. Chitnis, *The Scottish Enlightenment: a Social History* (London, 1976).

J.R.R. Christie, 'The origins and development of the Scottish scientific community, 1680–1760', *History of Science* 12 (1974).

E.A.G. Clark, 'The superiority of the "Scotch system": Scottish ragged schools and their influence', *Scottish Educational Studies* 9 (1977).

H. Corr, 'Politics of the sexes in English and Scottish teachers' unions, 1870–1914', in H. Corr and L. Jamieson, eds., *Politics of Everyday Life: Continuity and Change in Work and the Family* (London, 1990).

H. Corr, 'Dominies and domination: schoolteachers, masculinity and women in 19th century Scotland', *History Workshop Journal* 40 (1995).

J. Craigie, *A Bibliography of Scottish Education before 1872* (London, 1970).

J. Craigie, *A Bibliography of Scottish Education 1872–1972* (London, 1974).

J. Crawford, 'Reading and book use in 18th-century Scotland', *The Bibliotheck* 19 (1994).

M. Cruickshank, 'The Dick Bequest: the effect of a famous nineteenth-century endowment on parish schools of north east Scotland', *History of Education Quarterly* 5 (1965).

M. Cruickshank, 'The Argyll Commission report, 1865–8: a landmark in Scottish education', *British Journal of Educational Studies* 15 (1967).

M. Cruickshank, *A History of the Training of Teachers in Scotland* (London, 1970).

J. Darragh, 'The Apostolic Visitations of Scotland, 1912 and 1917', *Innes Review* 41 (1990).

G.E. Davie, *The Democratic Intellect: Scotland and her Universities in the Nineteenth Century* (2nd ed., Edinburgh, 1964).

G.E. Davie, *The Crisis of the Democratic Intellect: the Problem of Generalism and Specialisation in Twentieth-Century Scotland* (Edinburgh, 1986).

G.E. Davie, *The Scottish Enlightenment and Other Essays* (Edinburgh, 1991).

A. Doig and others, eds., *William Cullen and the Eighteenth Century Medical World* (Edinburgh, 1993).

I. Donnachie and G. Hewitt, *Historic New Lanark: the Dale and Owen Industrial Community since 1785* (Edinburgh, 1993).

D. Dow and M. Moss, 'The medical curriculum at Glasgow in the early nineteenth century', *History of Universities* 7 (1988).

D. Duncan, 'Scholarship and politeness in the early eighteenth century', in A. Hook, ed., *The History of Scottish Literature. Volume 2. 1660–1800* (Aberdeen, 1987).

V.E. Durkacz, 'Gaelic education in the nineteenth century', *Scottish Educational Studies* 9 (1977).

V.E. Durkacz, *The Decline of the Celtic Languages: a Study of Linguistic and Cultural Conflict in Scotland, Wales and Ireland from the Reformation to the Twentieth Century* (Edinburgh, 1983).

J. Durkan, 'Education in the century of the Reformation', *Innes Review* 10 (1959).

J. Durkan, 'Education: the laying of fresh foundations', in J. MacQueen, ed., *Humanism in Renaissance Scotland* (Edinburgh, 1990).

J. Durkan and J. Kirk, *The University of Glasgow 1451–1577* (Glasgow, 1977).

R.L. Emerson, 'Scottish universities in the eighteenth century, 1690–1800', *Studies on Voltaire and the Eighteenth Century* 167 (1977).

R.L. Emerson, 'Science and the origins and concerns of the Scottish Enlightenment', *History of Science* 26 (1988).

R.L. Emerson, *Professors, Patronage and Politics: the Aberdeen Universities in the Eighteenth Century* (Aberdeen, 1992).

R. Feenstra, 'Scottish–Dutch legal relations in the 17th and 18th centuries', in T.C. Smout, ed., *Scotland and Europe 1200–1850* (Edinburgh, 1986).

H. Ferguson, *Glasgow School of Art: the History* (Glasgow, 1995).

J. Fewell and F. Paterson, eds., *Girls in their Prime: Scottish Education Revisited* (Edinburgh, 1990).

T.A. Fitzpatrick, 'Catholic education in Glasgow, Lanarkshire and South-West Scotland before 1872', *Innes Review* 36 (1985).

T.A. Fitzpatrick, *Catholic Secondary Education in South-West Scotland before 1972: its Contribution to the Change in Status of the Catholic Community of the Area* (Aberdeen, 1986).

A.G. Fraser, *The Building of Old College: Adam Playfair & the University of Edinburgh* (Edinburgh, 1989).

W.H. Fraser and R.J. Morris, eds., *People and Society in Scotland. II. 1830–1914* (Edinburgh, 1990).

R. French, 'Medical teaching in Aberdeen: from the foundation of the University to the middle of the seventeenth century', *History of Universities* 3 (1983).

R.T.D. Glaister, 'Rural private teachers in 18th-century Scotland', *Journal of Educational Administration and History* 23 (1991).

Glasgow Women's Studies Group, *Uncharted Lives: Extracts from Scottish Women's Experiences, 1850–1982* (Glasgow, 1983).

J. Gray, A. McPherson and D. Raffe, *Reconstructions of Secondary Education: Theory, Myth and Practice since the War* (London, 1983).

S. Hamilton, 'The first generations of university women', in G. Donaldson, ed., *Four Centuries: Edinburgh University Life, 1583–1983* (Edinburgh, 1983).

A.W. Harding, 'Gaelic schools in northern Perthshire, 1823–1849', *Transactions of the Gaelic Society of Inverness* 52 (1980–2).

J.D. Hargreaves, *Academe and Empire: Some Overseas Connections of Aberdeen University, 1860–1970* (Aberdeen, 1994).

J.D. Hargreaves and A. Forbes, eds., *Aberdeen University 1945–1981:Regional Roles and National Needs* (Aberdeen, 1989).

M.M. Harrison and W.B. Marker, eds., *Teaching the Teachers: the History of Jordanhill College of Education, 1828–1993* (Edinburgh, 1996).

C. Harvie, 'The Folk and the *Gwerin*: the myth and the reality of popular culture in 19th-century Scotland and Wales', *Proceedings of the British Academy* 80 (1991).

J. Highet, *A School of One's Choice: a Sociological Study of the Fee-Paying Schools of Scotland* (London, 1969).

P. Hillis, 'Education and evangelisation: presbyterian missions in mid-nineteenth century Glasgow', *Scottish Historical Review* 66 (1987).

A. Hook and R.B. Sher, eds., *The Glasgow Enlightenment* (East Linton, 1995).

D.B. Horn, 'The Universities (Scotland) Act of 1858', *University of Edinburgh Journal* 19 (1958–60).

D.B. Horn, *A Short History of the University of Edinburgh, 1556–1889* (Edinburgh, 1967).

R.A. Houston, 'The literacy myth?: illiteracy in Scotland, 1630–1760', *Past and Present* 96 (1982).

R.A. Houston, 'Literacy and society in the West, 1500–1850', *Social History* 8 (1983).

R.A. Houston, *Scottish Literacy and the Scottish Identity: Illiteracy and Society in Scotland and Northern England, 1600–1800* (Cambridge, 1985).

R.A. Houston, *Literacy in Early Modern Europe: Culture and Education, 1500–1800* (London, 1988).

R.A. Houston, 'Scottish education and literacy, 1600–1800: an international perspective', in T.M. Devine, ed., *Improvement and Enlightenment* (Edinburgh, 1989).

R.A. Houston, 'Literacy, education and the culture of print in Enlightenment Edinburgh', *History* 78 (1993).

R.A. Houston and R.E. Tyson, 'The geography of literacy in Aberdeenshire in the early eighteenth century', *Journal of Historical Geography* 17 (1991).

W.M. Humes, *The Leadership Class in Scottish Education* (Edinburgh, 1986).

W.M. Humes and H. Paterson, eds., *Scottish Culture and Scottish Education, 1800–1980* (Edinburgh, 1983).

H. Hutchison, 'Church, state and school in Clackmannanshire, 1803–1872', *Scottish Educational Studies* 3 (1971).

I.G.C. Hutchison, *A Political History of Scotland, 1832–1924: Parties, Elections and Issues* (Edinburgh, 1986).

I.G.C. Hutchison, *The University and the State: the Case of Aberdeen, 1860–1963* (Aberdeen, 1993).

L. Jamieson and C. Toynbee, *Country Bairns: Growing Up, 1900–1930* (Edinburgh, 1992).

J.C. Jessop, *Education in Angus: an Historical Survey of Education up to the Act of 1872, from Original and Contemporary Sources* (London, 1931).

P. Jones, 'The polite academy and the Presbyterians, 1720–1770', in J. Dwyer and others, eds., *New Perspectives on the Politics and Culture of Early Modern Scotland* (Edinburgh, n.d.).

P. Jones, 'The Scottish professoriate and the polite academy, 1720–46', in I. Hont and M. Ignatieff, eds., *Wealth and Virtue: the Shaping of Political Economy in the Scottish Enlightenment* (Cambridge, 1983).

H. Kearney, *Scholars and Gentlemen: Universities and Society in Pre-Industrial Britain, 1500–1700* (London, 1970).

C.M. Kendall, 'Higher education and the emergence of the professional woman in Glasgow, c.1890–1914', *History of Universities* 10 (1991).

Brother Kenneth, 'The Education (Scotland) Act, 1918, in the making', *Innes Review* 19 (1968).

J. Kirk, ' "Melvillian" reform in the Scottish universities', in A.A. MacDonald and others, eds., *The Renaissance in Scotland: Studies in Literature, Religion, History and Culture Offered to John Durkan* (Leiden, 1994).

H.M. Knox, *Two Hundred and Fifty Years of Scottish Education, 1696–1946* (Edinburgh, 1953).

A. Law, *Education in Edinburgh in the Eighteenth Century* (London, 1965).

C. Lawrence, 'Ornate physicians and learned artisans: Edinburgh medical men, 1726–1776', in W.F. Bynum and R. Porter, eds., *William Hunter and the Eighteenth-Century Medical World* (Cambridge, 1985).

C. Lawrence, 'The Edinburgh medical school and the end of the "old thing", 1790–1830', *History of Universities* 7 (1988).

L. Leneman, *Living in Atholl: a Social History of the Estates, 1685–1785* (Edinburgh, 1986).

B. Lenman and J. Stocks, 'The beginnings of state education in Scotland, 1872–1885', *Scottish Educational Studies* 4 (1972).

J. Lloyd, 'The Second World War and educational aspiration: some Scottish evidence', *Journal of Educational Administration and History* 15 (1983).

J. Lloyd, 'Tom Johnston's parliament on education: the birth of the Sixth Advisory Council on Education in Scotland, 1942–43', *Scottish Educational Review* 16 (1984).

J. Lloyd, 'Educational gains and losses in the Second World War: a Scottish perspective', *History of Education* 21 (1992a).

J. Lloyd, 'The Scottish school system, educational reform and the Second World War', in R. Lowe, ed., *Education and the Second World War: Studies in Schooling and Social Change* (London, 1992b).

M. Lynch, 'The origins of Edinburgh's "toun college": a revision article', *Innes Review* 33 (1982).

L.J. Macfarlane, *William Elphinstone and the Kingdom of Scotland, 1431–1514: the Struggle for Order* (Aberdeen, 1985).

D.I. Mackay, *Geographical Mobility and the Brain Drain: a Case Study of Aberdeen University Graduates, 1860–1960* (London, 1969).

J.D. Mackie, *The University of Glasgow, 1451–1951: a Short History* (Glasgow, 1954).

P. Mackie, 'The foundation of the United Industrial School of Edinburgh: "A bold experiment"', *Innes Review* 39 (1988).

P. Mackie, 'Inter-denominational education and the United Industrial School of Edinburgh, 1847–1900', *Innes Review* 43 (1992).

K.M. MacKinnon, 'Education and social control: the case of Gaelic Scotland', *Scottish Educational Studies* 4 (1972).

M. Macleod, 'Gaelic in highland education', *Transactions of the Gaelic Society of Inverness* 43 (1960–3).

J.A. Mangan and C. Loughlan, 'Fashion and fealty: the Glaswegian bourgeoisie, middle-class schools and the games-ethic in the Victorian and Edwardian eras', *International Journal of the History of Sport* 5 (1988).

T.A. Markus, 'The school as machine: working class Scottish education and the Glasgow Normal Seminary', in T.A. Markus, ed., *Order in Space and Society: Architectural Form and its Context in the Scottish Enlightenment* (Edinburgh, 1982).

D.M. Mason, 'School attendance in nineteenth-century Scotland', *Economic History Review* 2nd series 38 (1985).

W.M. Mathew, 'The origins and occupations of Glasgow students, 1740–1839', *Past and Present* 33 (1966).

D. McCrone, *Understanding Scotland: the Sociology of a Stateless Nation* (London, 1992).

I.J. McDonald, 'Untapped reservoirs of talent? Social class and opportunities in Scottish higher education, 1910–1960', *Scottish Educational Studies* 1 (1967).

J. McGloin, 'Catholic education in Ayr, 1823–1918', *Innes Review* 13 (1962).

C.A. McLaren, 'Affrichtment and riot: student violence at Aberdeen, 1659–1669', *Northern Scotland* 10 (1990).

C.A. McLaren, 'The College and the community, 1600–1860', in J.S. Smith, ed., *Old Aberdeen: Bishops, Burghers and Buildings* (Aberdeen, 1991).

A. McPherson, 'The generally educated Scot: an old ideal in a changing university structure', in A. McPherson and others, eds., *Eighteen-Plus: the Final Selection* (Bletchley, 1972).

A. McPherson, 'Selections and survivals: a sociology of the ancient Scottish universities', in R. Brown, ed., *Knowledge, Education and Cultural Change: Papers in the Sociology of Education* (London, 1973).

A. McPherson, 'Schooling', in T. Dickson and J.H. Treble, eds., *People and Society in Scotland. III. 1914–1990* (Edinburgh, 1992).

A. McPherson and C.D. Raab, *Governing Education: a Sociology of Policy since 1945* (Edinburgh, 1988).

61

A. McPherson and J.D. Willms, 'Certification, class conflict, religion, and community: a socio-historical explanation of the effectiveness of contemporary schools', *Research in Sociology of Education and Socialization* 6 (1986).

G. Mercer and D.J.C. Forsyth, 'Some aspects of recruitment to school teaching among university graduates in Scotland, 1860–1955', *British Journal of Educational Studies* 23 (1975).

L. Moore, 'The Aberdeen Ladies' Educational Association, 1877–1883', *Northern Scotland* 3 (1977–80).

L. Moore, 'Aberdeen and the higher education of women, 1868–1877', *Aberdeen University Review* 48 (1979–80).

L. Moore, 'Invisible scholars: girls learning Latin and mathematics in the elementary public schools of Scotland before 1872', *History of Education* 13 (1984).

L. Moore, *Bajanellas and Semilinas: Aberdeen University and the Education of Women, 1860–1920* (Aberdeen, 1991).

L. Moore, 'Educating for the "woman's sphere": domestic training versus intellectual discipline', in E. Breitenbach and E. Gordon, eds., *Out of Bounds: Women in Scottish Society, 1800–1945* (Edinburgh, 1992).

J.B. Morrell, 'The University of Edinburgh in the late eighteenth century: its scientific eminence and academic structure', *Isis* 62 (1971).

J.B. Morrell, 'Science and Scottish university reform: Edinburgh in 1826', *British Journal for the History of Science* 6 (1972–3).

J.B. Morrell, 'The Edinburgh Town Council and its university, 1717–1766', in R.G.W. Anderson and A.D.C. Simpson, eds., *The Early Years of the Edinburgh Medical School* (Edinburgh, 1976).

J.D. Myers, 'Scottish nationalism and the antecedents of the 1872 Education Act', *Scottish Educational Studies* 4 (1972).

D.J. Northcroft, '"Secondary education" and the rhetoric of change', *Scottish Educational Review* 24 (1992).

R. O'Day, *Education and Society, 1500–1800: the Social Foundations of Education in Early Modern Britain* (London, 1982).

G.S. Osborne, *Scottish and English Schools: a Comparative Survey of the Past Fifty Years* (London, 1966).

L. Paterson, 'Liberation or control: what are the Scottish education traditions of the twentieth century?', in T.M. Devine and R.J. Finlay, eds., *Scotland in the Twentieth Century* (Edinburgh, 1996).

D.G. Paz, *The Politics of Working-Class Education in Britain, 1830–50* (Manchester, 1980).

C. Pennington, *The Modernisation of Medical Teaching at Aberdeen in the Nineteenth Century* (Aberdeen, 1994).

N.T. Phillipson, 'Culture and society in the 18th century province: the case of Edinburgh and the Scottish Enlightenment', in L. Stone, ed., *The University in Society. II. Europe, Scotland, and the United States from the 16th to the 20th Century* (Princeton, 1974).

N.T. Phillipson, 'The Scottish Enlightenment', in R. Porter and M. Teich, eds., *The Enlightenment in National Context* (Cambridge, 1981).

N.T. Phillipson, 'Commerce and culture: Edinburgh, Edinburgh University, and the Scottish Enlightenment', in T. Bender, ed., *The University and the City, from Medieval Origins to the Present* (New York, 1988).

N.T. Phillipson, ed., *Universities, Society, and the Future* (Edinburgh, 1983).

A.G. Ralston, 'The development of reformatory and industrial schools in Scotland, 1832–1872', *Scottish Economic and Social History* 8 (1988).

K. Robbins, *Nineteenth-Century Britain: Integration and Diversity* (Oxford, 1988).

A.F.B. Roberts, 'Scotland and infant education in the nineteenth century', *Scottish Educational Studies* 4 (1972).

P.L. Robertson, 'Scottish universities and Scottish industry, 1860–1914', *Scottish Economic and Social History* 4 (1984).

P.L. Robertson, 'The development of an urban university: Glasgow 1860–1914', *History of Education Quarterly* 30 (1990).

L. Rosner, *Medical Education in the Age of Improvement: Edinburgh Students and Apprentices, 1760–1826* (Edinburgh, 1991).

J.M. Roxburgh, *The School Board of Glasgow, 1873–1919* (London, 1971).

J.A. Russell, *History of Education in the Stewartry of Kirkcudbright, from Original and Contemporary Sources* (Newton Stewart, 1951).

J.A. Russell, *Education in Wigtownshire, 1560–1970* (Newton Stewart, 1971).

M. Sanderson, *The Universities and British Industry, 1850–1970* (London, 1972).

M. Sanderson, *The Universities in the Nineteenth Century* (London, 1975).

L.J. Saunders, *Scottish Democracy, 1815–1840: the Social and Intellectual Background* (Edinburgh, 1950).

J. Scotland, *The History of Scottish Education* (2 vols., London, 1969).

J. Scotland, 'The centenary of the Education (Scotland) Act of 1872', *British Journal of Educational Studies* 20 (1972).

S. Shapin, 'The audience for science in eighteenth century Edinburgh', *History of Science* 12 (1974).

R.B. Sher, *Church and University in the Scottish Enlightenment: the Moderate Literati of Edinburgh* (Edinburgh, 1985).

R.B. Sher, 'Commerce, religion and the Enlightenment in eighteenth-century Glasgow', in T.M. Devine and G. Jackson, eds., *Glasgow. Volume I. Beginnings to 1830* (Manchester, 1995).

I.J. Simpson, *Education in Aberdeenshire Before 1872* (London, 1947).

A. Slaven and D.W. Kim, 'The origins and economic and social roles of Scottish business leaders, 1860–1960', in T.M. Devine, ed., *Scottish Elites* (Edinburgh, 1994).

R.N. Smart, 'Some observations on the provinces of the Scottish universities, 1560–1850', in G.W.S. Barrow, ed., *The Scottish Tradition: Essays in Honour of Ronald Gordon Cant* (Edinburgh, 1974).

63

N. Smelser, *Social Paralysis and Social Change: British Working-Class Education in the Nineteenth Century* (Berkeley, 1991).

J.A. Smith, 'The 1872 Education (Scotland) Act and Gaelic education', *Transactions of the Gaelic Society of Inverness* 51 (1978–80).

T.C. Smout, *A History of the Scottish People, 1560–1830* (new ed., n.p., 1972).

T.C. Smout, 'Born again at Cambuslang: new evidence on popular religion and literacy in eighteenth-century Scotland', *Past and Present* 97 (1982).

T.C. Smout, *A Century of the Scottish People, 1830–1950* (London, 1986).

D. Southgate, *University Education in Dundee: a Centenary History* (Edinburgh, 1982).

W.B. Stephens, 'Literacy in England, Scotland, and Wales, 1500–1900', *History of Education Quarterly* 30 (1990).

D. Stevenson, *King's College, Aberdeen, 1560–1641: from Protestant Reformation to Covenanting Revolution* (Aberdeen, 1990).

M.A. Stewart, ed., *Studies in the Philosophy of the Scottish Enlightenment* (Oxford, 1990).

J. Stocks, 'The people versus the Department: the case of Circular 44', *Scottish Educational Review* 27 (1995).

L. Stone, 'Literacy and education in England, 1640–1900', *Past and Present* 42 (1969).

G. Sutherland, 'Education', in F.M.L. Thompson, ed., *The Cambridge Social History of Britain, 1750–1950. Volume III. Social Agencies and Institutions* (Cambridge, 1990).

A. Thomson, *Ferrier of St Andrews: an Academic Tragedy* (Edinburgh, 1985).

I. Thomson, 'The origins of physical education in state schools', *Scottish Educational Review* 10 (1978).

J.H. Treble, 'The development of Roman Catholic education in Scotland, 1878–1978', *Innes Review* 29 (1978).

J.H. Treble, 'The working of the 1918 Education Act in Glasgow archdiocese', *Innes Review* 31 (1980).

H.R. Trevor-Roper, 'The Scottish Enlightenment', *Studies on Voltaire and the Eighteenth Century* 58 (1967).

R.K. Webb, 'Literacy among the working classes in nineteenth century Scotland', *Scottish Historical Review* 33 (1954).

E.G. West, *Education and the Industrial Revolution* (London, 1975).

I.D. Whyte, *Scotland Before the Industrial Revolution: an Economic and Social History, c.1050–c.1750* (London, 1995).

C.W.J. Withers, *Gaelic in Scotland, 1698–1981: the Geographical History of a Language* (Edinburgh, 1984).

D.J. Withrington, 'The S.P.C.K. and Highland schools in mid-eighteenth century', *Scottish Historical Review* 41 (1962).

D.J. Withrington, 'Schools in the presbytery of Haddington in the 17th century', *Transactions of the East Lothian Antiquarian and Field Naturalists' Society* 9 (1963).

D.J. Withrington, 'The Free Church Educational Scheme, 1843–50', *Scottish Church History Society Records* 15 (1963–5).

D.J. Withrington, 'Lists of schoolmasters teaching Latin, 1690', in *Miscellany of the Scottish History Society. Volume X* (Edinburgh, 1965).

D.J. Withrington, 'Education and society in the eighteenth century', in N.T. Phillipson and R. Mitchison, eds., *Scotland in the Age of Improvement: Essays in Scottish History in the Eighteenth Century* (Edinburgh, 1970).

D.J. Withrington, 'Towards a national system, 1867–72: the last years in the struggle for a Scottish Education Act', *Scottish Educational Studies* 4 (1972).

D.J. Withrington, 'Education in the 17th century Highlands', in *The Seventeenth Century in the Highlands* (Inverness, 1986).

D.J. Withrington, ' "A ferment of change": aspirations, ideas and ideals in nineteenth-century Scotland', in D. Gifford, ed., *The History of Scottish Literature. Volume 3. Nineteenth Century* (Aberdeen, 1988a).

D.J. Withrington, 'Schooling, literacy and society', in T.M. Devine and R. Mitchison, eds., *People and Society in Scotland. I. 1760–1830* (Edinburgh, 1988b).

D.J. Withrington, 'The Scottish universities: living traditions? old problems renewed?', in *The Scottish Government Yearbook 1992* (Edinburgh, 1992).

D.J. Withrington, 'Adrift among the reefs of conflicting ideals? Education and the Free Church, 1843–55', in S.J. Brown and M. Fry, eds., *Scotland in the Age of the Disruption* (Edinburgh, 1993).

P. Wood, 'Science and the Aberdeen Enlightenment', in P. Jones, ed., *Philosophy and Science in the Scottish Enlightenment* (Edinburgh, 1988).

P. Wood, 'The scientific revolution in Scotland', in R. Porter and M. Teich, eds., *The Scientific Revolution in National Context* (Cambridge, 1992).

P. Wood, *The Aberdeen Enlightenment: the Arts Curriculum in the Eighteenth Century* (Aberdeen, 1993).

P. Wood, 'Science, the universities and the public sphere in eighteenth-century Scotland', *History of Universities* 13 (1994).

C.J. Wright, 'Academics and their aims: English and Scottish approaches to university education in the nineteenth century', *History of Education* 8 (1979).